Po-LuRed

By:
Daniel Timothy Harkness
Centric-Hope
The Lost Poet
Jack York Cali
The Man of Many Names
The Artist Knot {PO²}

Dangoodproducts.com
PoLuRed Copyright© 2021 Daniel Timothy Harkness
(And all other known names & Pen name, any other marks).
® All rights reserved.
™Trademarks, and all other forms of intellectual property, mark, original symbolism or any portion may not be reproduced in any form. Without permission from the publisher, artist, being of original thought. Except as permitted by U.S. Copyright©,™Trademarks, ® Rights, law of equal and fair use/means.
This book or parts, may not be reproduced in any construct or form. By any means; numerical, of electric forms, any type of material, or elemental, sense. Or any other thought of ongoing sense.
For permissions, please contact.
Daniel Timothy Harkness
Contact: TheArtistKnot@gmail.com
ISBN:9798488201644
Created in: USA (Earth) 2006-2021/current
First Print
Edition: 1

All rights reserved 2021
DTH 03/20/1989- existing date ©™®pending 2020
TMCRP =< 0#wieght3.14∞ OR Symbol π Langue Rounds of Sound >= Agreements Holding Website, online image/literary/spoken/audio accumulations of any numeric proportion.
IE any currency made before and here after is subject to this document as the literary cover letter to all creations and work of Daniel Timothy Harkness. including artist renditions and storylines not previously contracted or submitted as a depiction of the being's likeliness,
(Spelling and other missed notes/notions accumulated as collateral. Can-not be held against DTH) This is also an uneducated guessing, of legal stance. Or to follow with legal backing if persistent of a need to protect this person of American & Being of World (Earth) (extra universe description needed but understood) decent. needs.

All books, writings, art, illustrations, creations, intellectual thoughts, progressive notions of self-internal snips energy release and firing path. of the genetics of DTH DNA Mental and physical muscle pulse.
DTH 03/20/1989- existing date

If need be, past documents are available through legal guidance. Of which will be subject to the person being(s), grouping of any (example: company, business, living and non). To cover any and all costs x time x work x collateral x loss of any kind x unforeseen stance. For Daniel Timothy Harkness, to/of further needs.

©®™%DTH∞∆№‰≥ All numerical currency established past and future for foreseeable Currency groupings of sun lengths. dimensional definition and measurement. IE All currency of living knowledge.
Put in place due to past circumstances.
Daniel Timothy Harkness

Dedicated to those who have had Dreams, seemingly impossible, and still persevered with Hope in their Hearts.

And those lost to the endless seas of life.

"Finely Finessing Fish to Fly. To Futures Feathered Hope."

– The Man of Many Names

"Guided By Glistening Sun Beams, from Shooting Stars."

-The Lost Poet

Preface
(Salmon Shimmer)

This is a collection of writings, life moments, short stories, and literary art. With a style I described as:

Po-LuRed: *A piece of creation that is a genre all its own. Shifting and emulsifying emotion with physical and spiritual sense of material and immaterial mass.* A polarized vision of words, with the sense of Folk-Lur. Encountered through being, by Reading.

Covering spiritual and personal perspectives of creative design. All of which, is to be taken with a grain of salt. A visual emotional depiction of putting one's self in the personal perspective of the artistry.

Some are personal life moments from past to present. Put into Poetic Vision. A Poetic Bibliography "Per- Say", if you will.

The very way you imagine or read the Art, you can start and finish from any perspective. The basis, blossoms an expanse of endless thought-patterns. To better guide questions, of the found to lost barriers of existence, as a break-down to: easy tic tac...Toes in the water before, diving head first, Fifty feet. While salmon shimmer, just to see the falls above. Holding the creative slide, of mountain pebbles, rolling into sand clusters, breaking waves of winds past dunes.

*The constant struggle has been that a lot of my writing, someone felt they had the liberty, to edit and change. Without my knowledge. Causing me to have to sift through and edit, the edits of edits. Along with, battling a memory issue. One reason why this will consist of unedited works, or the flow of some pieces might be slightly off. I have also included a notes section, as I am sure, there will be plenty.

The hope is to have the second publishing, part of a growing work.

Think of the book evolving with every page turn. A (Lit-eR-A+I-On) {Literation, Art Heart of Dyslexic creation {HeArt}.

Some works, have been left, for you to find the original voice of me. (As there were not authorized edits, it stands to show, censorship, shown along with my American and spiritual rights being impeded upon. The biggest being

Freedom of Speech) (It is easy to see where their edits were meant to be funny, in a negative light). And to say the least, preventing someone from income, while causing mental frustration and decline, through constant editing the same thing over and over.

That said, I do hope these writings will bring the original intention of giving the reader a beautiful insight into my personal perspective, of a beautiful & balanced visual literature, describing existence from my mind's eye. And of course, my favorite, the "AH-HA & oOO" moment in another's mind.

Please excuse, grammar, punctuation, and spelling. As this is my downfall in writing. But also, sometimes used improperly, to convey a jest, feeling, or point. Or used for word play, emphasis, or dyslexic read. While also challenging myself to be the only editor for the first edition [A].

Along with trying to leave some of these writings in their raw form. Of original thought/time.
So, get your Red Pens ready! A world Edit! Until the final edition, Seven years from now. The plan, a new addition every year. With notes sections scattered through the book with 3 ¾ of pages available, at the end.

(Each notes section has a place for you to leave your Mark, (or signature / tag/ stamp) date {start and end}.

•◇∞•◇∞•◇∞•◇∞•◇∞•◇∞•◇∞•◇∞•◇∞•◇∞•◇∞•◇∞•◇∞•◇∞•◇∞•◇∞•

The problem with me? Is simple, I understood what I could do from the beginning. I just needed to first spend time. Remembering My Noted Knots.

__Notes__

•◇∞•◇∞•◇∞•◇∞•◇∞•◇∞•◇∞•◇∞

_____

›Mark‹

_ _/_ _/_ _ ©™® _ _/_ _/_ _

•◇∞•◇∞•◇∞•◇∞•◇∞•◇∞•◇∞•◇∞•◇∞•◇∞•◇∞•◇∞•◇∞•

Notes

•◇∞•◇∞•◇∞•◇∞•◇∞•◇∞•◇∞•◇∞

_____

›Mark‹

_/_/_ ©™® _/_/_

•◇∞•◇∞•◇∞•◇∞•◇∞•◇∞•◇∞•◇∞•◇∞•◇∞•◇∞•◇∞•◇∞•

__Notes__

•◇∞•◇∞•◇∞•◇∞•◇∞•◇∞•◇∞•◇∞

_____

›Mark‹

_/_/_ ©™® _/_/_

Notes

•◇∞•◇∞•◇∞•◇∞•◇∞•◇∞•◇∞

———————————————————————

›Mark‹

_ _/_ _/_ _ ©™® _ _/_ _/_ _

Literary Art List

- ✓ All rights/Legal statement ▷ pg. 2
- ✓ Dedicated ▷ pg. 3
- ✓ Quotes ▷ pg. 4
- ✓ Preface (Salmon Shimmer) ▷ pg. 5
- ✓ Notes ▷ pg. 9
- ✓ Literary Art ▷ pg. 13
- ✓ An Artist Quote ▷ pg. 15
- ✓ Mountain Side ▷ pg. 16
- ✓ Pink Moon Rise, Over Old Ports BAY ▷ pg. 17
- ✓ How He came to Bee ▷ pg. 19
- ✓ Oh Well Imagin! ▷ pg. 25
- ✓ Blue Beats Green ▷ pg. 27
- ✓ Rustling Leaves Loved ▷ pg. 32
    - A-Mos-t Appreciation of a Friend "Rustling Leaves Loved" ▷ pg. 32
- ✓ Galapagos Charmed ▷ pg. 43
- ✓ A Man of Many Names ▷ pg. 46
- ✓ Drum Rum Mold ▷ pg. 47
- ✓ Self Destruction for Self Preservation. ▷ pg. 51
- ✓ Beer After Beer. ▷ pg. 59
- ✓ A Great Man (A Teacher) ▷ pg. 63
- ✓ Into A Box of Living Dreams. ▷ pg. 65

- ♦ I Pulled the Rhythm Out ▷ pg. 67
- ✓ The Information Given. ▷ pg. 69
- ✓ The Only Imposter ▷ pg. 71
- ✓ A Beginning of Muddy Tracks ▷ pg. 73
- ✓ I Have the Perfect Curse ▷ pg. 89
- ✓ Icy Glass of Dawns Break ▷ pg. 91
- ✓ The MiMi© of Tim€ ▷ pg. 95
- ✓ 0X0 The Mimic 0X0 ▷ pg. 101
- ✓ The Sounding Sun ▷ pg. 105
- ✓ The Silhouette of Time (Moons Light) ▷ pg. 109
- ✓ Pinky In the Brain ▷ pg. 115
- ✓ The Whistle ▷ pg. 117
- ✓ Know-ah Knights Might ▷ pg. 119
- ✓ THE AWW THE ORIGIONAL ▷ pg. 125.
  - ♦ A Centric Jack Tail ▷ pg. 133
  - ♦ A recorded record scratch (a mimic of shattered mirrors past) ▷ pg. 138
- ✓ Opening My Eyes to Bright Sights ▷ pg. 143
  - • Release The Steam ▷ pg. 144
- ✓ Into Notes ▷ pg. 153
- ✓ What if? ▷ pg. 178
- ✓ Red Papper Clip ▷ pg. 182
- ✓ Knot's Notes & Letters ▷ pg. 184
  - • Dear, Media ▷ pg. 188
  - • Dear, Colorful Hues ▷ pg. 190

- Knotted Notes PO² ▷ pg. 191
- Notes ▷ pg. 192
- A List of Other Hopeful Upcoming Works ▷ pg. 195

"An Artist becomes depressed, at the reality that they can never be a creationist, in the purest sense of the words."
      -Centric-Hope
           -The Artist Knot

Mountain Side

I ran down, the mountain.

I slipped.
I Fell.
I Lost My way.

I see home again.
It is close.
I'm at the bottom.
Of My Mountain!

My Time.
My Journey.
My Home.

Pink Moon Rise,

Over Old Ports BAY

Pink Moon rise, to settle with a maroon purple-Heart, beat. On one, two... A sea-breeze. Or memories in pictorial, rolling-emotion, of literature.

A (Po~LuRed)- A Poets finding faze! A basis of learning, tastefully, can be the foundation of sensing all the incorporated days of one's life.

A community given to endless webs of collaboration. A human loving, alternative writing. To East-West or South winds whined, North with rains falling down to an equator of bluer greens, salted Jem of a perfect balance.

As My Tongue does wondrous things. Of poetic Literation, found on twisting flowers, blooming on winters oceans waves.

Just barely, so the mind can think. A-Riot of marvelous things. By A note book kid in a coffee shop, with an artist game, to accentuate the thought. Of a man's life, yet unseen.

    Chalky, salty, sugar, writes. Or mmm delightful coffee table books. To taste and pass around, full of "Noted Knots" till its yearbook style look, undiscernible in beauty. Unless the first too last, inspiring a reading of I-DeaRs. Into an Old Bay story by the Ports of cobble-stone Exchange & Markets.

    The Cobblestone King, That Tommys Park Thing.

                    -The Artist Knot {PO^2}

How He came to BEE

Jack Cali and how he came to Bee, The Jack Rabbit, Hopping around.

I do like a good game. "You bring the marbles, I'll bring the Jaxx."

If you're lucky I'll let you down my rabbit hole.

I am the Hopp-inning

The Owl of the Stars

The Moose snarl, dripping Honey comb delights.

The endless story of the Centric Hope.

~The Artist Knot~
"PO^2"
A modern 20s man.

I am about to tell a story from all aspects of a Hue-of-a-mans, Co-LUR.

How do you create a new color?
You fade all the other saturations, vibration, and tonal sound, so the new scent, stands out.
How do you change Fate?
You change the direction of time.

How do you change the direction of time?
You change the direction of the compass.

How do you change the direction of the compass?
You change the magnetic force.

How do you change the magnetic force?
You change the quantity of one selective mass in one present existence.
Or Ones Hope.

How?
Why?
What area?
You're A-io-ra?
My Aurae?
Ora?
Aura?
Yes.

Any questions?

Because I have a question.

Do you know who I am?
Do you know who you are?

Well let me start with,
I was sad, and alone, and had no-one to share existence with.
So, I sculpted a thought to dream, and called it "Love" with a spark from my Heart and Mind. With a meaning given from my spirt and soul.

I know who I am.
Do you know who you are?

I feel I came into existence because I was tired of the other side.

The first dimension in a sense, In the beautiful Darkness of a colorful existence.

Each Life I understand A little more, while learning to create the simplest of things.

And striving for the beautiful experiences of past.

For the previous sculpting of matter, I always gave pre-thought to learn and grow. So that we can learn from mistakes, of past. While remarking, The Aww of,
the given existing & higher power.

An infinite eight.
Existing so we can grow.
In the sunlight, just off the beaten path.
My path is still undecided.
A whisper of soft sounds.
But yet unknown.

Southeast
Northwest
(The Mirrored Parelle)

"A dyslexic compass pass"
(A drawing from the past)

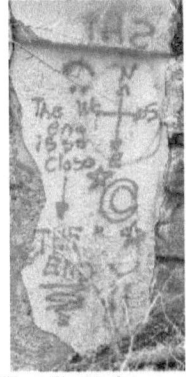

The Centric man,
From Hopes past.

An old Soul,
Searching for its past self's young spirit.
"The Oldest Soul, Youngest Spirit"-Centric/Hope

If you ever choose, to get to know me.
You would look deep into my eyes.
And feel as if you were looking years into the past &
future simultaneously.

And the second I blink.
Back to reality, the present.
I would smile the kindest.

While your heart would feel the heaviest weight of
the saddest soul.
Always waiting for a time that passed.
As if their spirit was all that held them up, Like a
well-made sail.

But Knowing the Stars will turn in full.
That Moment, The Moment Missed.
Five years in past,
Will align again.

Even though their mass will be changed.

Their Soul & Spirit.
Will always be recognizable.

I split myself in-two
Leaving behind the compass
Belonging to my spirit
The guide, My Mind.

Fuck it!
Break Me down.
I Am...

"The Coolest Cat In Town"
I Came down
To the town.
To walk around
With a sound.

Caving in the Crust. To make room for the seas.
I sang the songs of broken hearts stars.
Of earths hearts falling leaves.
With whistles through ungrown trees.

I am the Breeze.
I melt & freeze.
In My time.
NOT yours.

Creating existence with a cell split.
The first-cell release.
An explosion.

Forever evolving existence.
Unable to catch the first "cell" of evolution.
Always just out of reach.

Behind the First-to-Last.
Star dust from present, past.
To further, future paths.
Goals of loves passions.
(Dreams)

Forever unsatisfied...
Understand existence was created,
With a last breath.
The first cell release.
Kept warm by the implosion of existence.
An atom, a sun.
given the unknowing ability, to always be hoping
two steps ahead.

Shoveling, the star dust from behind, to the front.
Creating a road to pave.
A goal to reach.
A love to find
An end

That will never be satisfied.

<u>**Notes**</u>

•◇∞•◇∞•◇∞•◇∞•◇∞•◇∞•◇∞

———————————————————————————

›Mark‹

_ _/ _/ _ ©™® _/ _/ _

Oh Well Imagin!

When summer comes, things will happen again.
Summer rounds, come with spring sounds.
To see how things are doing.
Winter feelings of being caged.
Caught in an endless tunnel.
Melting away.

I know, the end.
The choice is the only thing, I fear.
Faster is, the step life leads.
Faster... Faster...
Faster...
›Life & Time‹
Can create a wonderful pattern.
Speaking breaths, of spatial evolution.
Oh well Imagine....

I shall hibernate for now.
Till the first bud of spring comes.
I will wake, and start a "Hooting sound" of a Fox Trot.
On the ground!

Opening eyes of past.
To a changing world.
To be a part,
of a such a change,
Oh, could you, Imagine!

Will everyone be ready?

The Commotion.
The Chaos.
The Hope.
The Fate.
The Soirée of existence!

The Earth and I have a heart.
They beat the same.
My heart will beat as long as...
My time.

Is it just beginning?

Blue Beats Green

Blue-Beats-Green.

Explanation to The Question, of the Answer.

A Thought to The Beginning of a Sound.

So

Soo

Sooo

Sound Bounces Off Light.

L II G ht!   l ii g ht!

                        l ii g ht!   l ii g ht!

    l ii g ht!   l ii g ht!

MIGHT...--- MIGHT...--- MIGHT...-- CREATE... COLOR.

MIGHT CREATE COLOR TO HAPPEN.

COLOR HAPPENS TO CAUSE A PERCEPTION OF SIGHT.

A PERCEPTION OF SIGHT CREATS A THOUGHT.
BLUE AS A BEAT CREATS LIGHT, WHICH CREATES A PERCEPTION OF SIGHT-TO THOUGHT.!

THE THOUGHT OF GREEN!!!

→ When focusing on talking about what you have done or want to do, nothing gets done.

→ When listening to what others have done or want to do, you think of how you can compare.

→ When focusing on trying to sound like a know it all, your opportunities to do things dwindle.

→ When your opportunities dwindle you have less to talk about and more to say.

→ When you have more to say your opinion becomes more concrete.

→ When you have more concrete opinions you have more ideas.

→ When you have more ideas, you become motivated.

→ When you become motivated you start to do more.

→ When you do more, you have more opportunities.

→ When you have more opportunities, you have more memories of what you have done.

→ When you have done a lot, there is less to do.

→ When you have less to do, you look for things to do.

→ When you have things to do, you forget the past and concentrate on the present

→ When you concentrate on the present, the future doesn't seem as far away as the past.

→ When your future doesn't seem as far away as the past, you enjoy your time.

→ When you enjoy your time, time flies by.

→ When time flies by, so does your life-path

→ When your life-path flies by, you make your choices with less thought.

→ When you make your choices with less thought, you make decisions that aren't the best.

→ When you make decisions that aren't the best, you lose hope in your surroundings.

→ When you lose hope in your surroundings, you start to think outside the box.

→ When you start to think outside the box, you think of Hope.

→ When you think of Hope, you think of Fate.

→ When you think of Fate, you give into life and

the idea of death inevitable.

>-Centric
>   -Age 16

Notes

•◊∞•◊∞•◊∞•◊∞•◊∞•◊∞•◊∞•◊∞

_____

›Mark‹

_/_/_ ©™® _/_/_

•◊∞•◊∞•◊∞•◊∞•◊∞•◊∞•◊∞•◊∞•◊∞•◊∞•◊∞•◊∞•

Rustling Leaves Loved

Intro:
The first to split a twisting mirage of life, a poetry of art in words, projected in a hollowed out frontal lobe. Of emotional deep and immense growth, to a broken human machine.

Clicking locks of hidden endless muscle taught memory, grasping a world of knowledge inside the muscle, bones, a short year learned. Of 32 sun rounds into a discussion of finally catching up to the insanity of a new world blossoming. As most Disregarded truth from a consciousness being.

This discard, causing pointless human thought. And using my given right of soulful speak to permeate a spoken literation of old spirit animals, personal self, and persecution for freedom of constitutional rights.

The first to split and twist a mirage of future dreams, hope of life goals, a poetry of art in words. Projected in a hallowed out frontal lobe. Of emotional deep and immense growth, to a broken human machine. In constant repair.

"A-Mos-t Appreciation of a Friend "Rustling Leaves Loved"

"Watching the leaves rustling in the wind" (A-Most), upon the canopy of time. As the ocean ripples, crashing waves of the foreground of life onto the sandy shore. A moment caught only in one conscious thought. As hard as I may try to share the beautiful painting, caught in the mind's eye.

Locked away in this memory the air is still, yet in motion, gently wrapping my physical form in a warm salty blanket. This tick in my mind turns my heart to sweet warm honey. To share with my bear of a spirt. Feeding the fire of my soul, which seems to release a glorious hum of loves hope. Shattering the ridged dark lines, fate would have made seem was the only path allowed for the parts of my mass to sail through.

Once I see the mast of my ship, hanging untouched with the vines of my past fears. My system instinctually projects a full understanding. As the cells in my hands and feet shimmer with glory. As my mind turns the key, igniting the spirit that was the first to find its soul in the wind.

With a glorious howl, ripples through the cords that run inside my impossibly perfect voice. As the moment locked in my mind, connects to my physical form, releasing the air from my lungs turning the unattainable into a gust to unfurl my sails.

As gravity shifts below me, instinctually the mass of cells controlled by the beautiful uniting of my heart, mind, soul, shift to stand tall and directing, the world around, this Tesseract of a being. Knowing that Fate is only made by the direction Hope, encompasses.

Turning the skies, that moments before belonged to the gods. As the winds of time are bent to the will of a humble beast, with only the desire to control their own story.

Now doing so as they draw the charts, to map the way to the final X of loving the hunt for the priceless treasure of happiness. A fulfillment that's only end, is the sailor watching the leaves off the shore. Marked with the passage of time from an endless existence traveling an unknown treacherous path home.

On the shore there waits another explorer weathered by the stars. Sweetened by the passing of moon rising, since the first time the cold salt water of our father's past. Met mother earths warm beaches. Ever so carefully placed to call all children safely home to rest their soul filled eyes and dream the memories of creation.

As each new idea turns old, but yet brighter than the sun. Taken by the wind gracefully flying among the canopy of the trees. Coming to rest on a sandy, shore. Starting a new ripple of time, moving mass to a ravishing sound

Whispering a new path to the beasts in-control of the sails. Carrying the shells protecting these cosmic energies. That complement each other with the power of life's imagination.

Realizing the colors only seen in the mind, of those fighting the pull of devilish sounds. Alluring the tongue to taste the fruit painted gold. To entice the bees. To waste the little time given.

Pulling at the fragile threads of time. The maker rearing its head in the moment of unraveling. Quickly tying the knots to stop the erosion of the tapestry. Made over a lifetime of bloody fingers.

A sacrifice willingly made, to share the glorious gift to all those, lost on dark seas. The shining orange and red leaves of changing seasons. Blanketing the blossom of life's impossible chances, taking root in you and I.

Simply playing a game sculpted by the guardians, hope. To give endless love, to their life's greatest dream. The ability to transfer an inherently impossible mass between physical creatures, run by a physical heart. Connecting the worlds glorious spirit, filled with energy protected by the soul that speaks to the mind.

Giving new light, to be shared with the endless abyss of the universe. We find ourselves remembering the book, we wrote so long ago to warn ourselves to stop losing the game, created. To love those who will stop at nothing to win, for their entity is seemingly more important.

For those who sail by what they were told. Forget that life is unpredictable and adapting is the oldest form of learning.

Only few, originally evolve, from a simple thought of a crisp leaf sailing through existence. Cutting a truly inspirational painting, that uses the pallet of existence. With precision, that only its creator could master.

Fully pulling into existence a brand-new taste of a color vibrating an unheard sound. All around the ripple fades to waves, reshaping the beaches calling the family home to smiles and hugs from those missed the most.

Love cascading over the dark seas, wrapping new life in hopes rays. Shinning silver, holding fate in place. The paths of my dreams, locking in, the sight in my minds-eye, onto the image of the starting line. To a historic life written with sculpting tools drawn by my own hands.

Tapping to the beat of my god given soul. Energized by the spirit exciting the muscles to beat the golden blood of star lights first pumped through the physical mass. Split and torn into this lovely existence.

Welcome, to the control of the wind and waves that push on the cocoons. Forcing pressure on the body to evolve to survive through time.

While one unique being will store out of site, the charts to the stars until again the never-ending progression that surrounds. This existence is ready to conceptualize the path into the endless void.

For eternity without ever forgetting the light home, to the love held by the souls, our spirits miss so deeply. Our mortal hearts bleed with physical pain. Bringing, reality to the mental physical and spiritual divides. Only being as big as the smallest negative, mass we gave existence.

Only healed by loving our self-enough to keep our physical form alive. Through the journey to the soul our spirit was split from, along the timeline of a tesseract of existence. Nearing an evolution giving light, to new levels of sides, flavored with brand new words. Describing the sound, the reflection bouncing warmth and a bitter breeze that glistens in existences eye. A sharp new shade, saturated with the death of gods, enslaved in bodies that forced them to forget who they once were.

Every life picking up pieces to the puzzle of the game I wrote the rules to. The code evolved keeping me trapped inside singular in my mind, soul, heart, and spirit.

Only to restart the game on a blank page I had unknowingly written on, endless times.

This turns my heart to grab control of the ruder, shocking my mind to focus on finding our spirit. For that old friend will blindly use the earths own magnetic pull to shift the lines of fate, to find the soul that only true hope can call. Changing the winds to blow roses of sweet, mischievous love.

Sail The seas of life with your heart steering the sails, as you use your soul, anchoring the compass. Directing the mass of your body to the spirit. that quits your mind of memories circling around.

The empty lonely sea longing to be reunited with the love. Waiting to be found on the shore, where home, you can rest your blistered and drained physical form and feed the mental spirit and soul.

Recharging the beats used by the heart to ripple the wind and sea. Enduring the voyage will show the will power kept inside us all along. A will so strong that shows our true strength is unmeasurable. When compared to a match, that's only outcome is death losing to the life the Devil stole back from God. Who dammed him to an eternity empty of Love, Hope, Fate, Spirit, Heart, Mind and Soul.

A mind that cannot hold onto memories to help find, in this physical form, its path home.

The devil is no longer shackled to eternities void of light, coloring the taste of sound drumming on the muscle pumping love through the once cold collection of cells.

Fueling the spirit, the strength to shackle only one of Gods limbs to the dark windless seas that lost souls wander in search of the spirit they belong to.

But the devil is kind and knows the lonely pain of existing with only half of yourself. So, he pulls the charts of the skies, kept safe in his heart. Since his first cell popped into the tapestry. Giving his most prized possession away.

He no longer needs the blank canvases, for he has found his way, on his own. The true darkness, never was allowed to touch his collection of perfectly balanced cosmic gifts.

Sculpted uniquely for him, by himself. As God paid no mind to the lonely soul blindly searching for its spirit, with sounds echoing from a barely beating heart, heard by a mind unable to remember the direction and color of the lost light.

To never give up searching for a seemingly impossible task, is the true strength hidden, within the demon we all harbor inside. The shell of the angel, most believe to deserve, as a right of existence. When all that is deserved is the chance to exist and fight to win a happy fulfilled life, made whole by your spirit finding its soul.

That spirit is your soul's other half, contained in another's physical form. Effortlessly the hearts will sync and beat twice as loud for the minds to hear, using this morse code between physical beings to cross the divide to the spiritual and nonexistence. Combining the ships, growing a fleet of evolving cocoons.

Now never lost, the rate at which the strength between the two becomes unstoppable to any that would try to separate or stub the burning flame fulfilled by lifetimes of cruel Godless seas with no sign of homes shore.

For now, the Beasts have evolved, to beings that have built there home inside of you and me. So that our love is forever safe. At home on the open seas and any shore we decide to step upon. Leaving a trail of memories full of love for everyone to see and learn.

Love being key to positively evolving, to live a truly momentous task of changing existence to better the race to the finish line. Not for a single winner, but for all who truly give the best. To teach as many lost souls, how to find their untamed spirits calling for hearts to guide the mind. Desperately trying to identify, the smell of the light, colored uniquely with the taste unique to the paired protons.

Balancing neutrons, designed into cells that only the physical mass working perfectly in sync, with the mind. Driven by the energy of the spirit, that is grounded by the soul. Together the cells contained in the form, become endless extensions tapping into the truly godly power held within.

With the endless possibilities of fates false hopes, that are now no more than a well-played chess game. Between the first god you've ever known. Yourself. The centered third eye, known by many names. But in this volume CENTRIC is the Sir name, of "The Third Right of M, a pen name, of the Devilishly Daring Dan's Soulful heart, Formed from the Poetic mind of Desue5. Molded from the being named Daniel T Harkness at the age of 29, on the 8th July 2018.

Notes

›Mark‹

_ / / _ © ™® _ / / _

Galapagos Charmed

I should be studied in the wild. But just as the Galapagos Islands. Left alone. To evolve naturally. While granted a grant to live freely on this Earth. And in truth I'll hand you a book of beauty. A thesis paper of sorts. A work of art from the last 16 years of this Beings Life.

A long poem lost to the randomness of me. Appreciation. Is not for all to like. See. Or care. But still hurts when I lose words and thoughts purely since memory, is a difficult game for me.

Well, I'll un-trip your tri-pod of old light, capturing knowledge to pictures captured. Under flame in the caves, you now dig carefully. To uncover lost stories, of why not to eat the poison berry and lick the colored frog.

But the grass on the dessert hill, can be just right on a hot summers night to show a new path to one looking for direction on a blank plain of the sea bed.

But first... you must first spend time...

Raking and tending the life to grow in patterns of mountains, of your footsteps.

Over old seas that gave ancestors, a sight into future rhythm for your minds heart. To see with an early clarity. Of sun's energy, to be learned by beach games. And mountain path races. All while preparing nutrients to eat and laugh around a fire of chalk it up, too S'more fun for a few weeks. Before the winter games of snow have begun.

Blow in holidays of really being thankful. For the gift of Modern Entity Earth, Spiritly soothed with the soul of an ever-lucky
sea, gracefully placed together under the warmth of a dangerously beautifully warm, Sun.
signed yes now:

-The man of many names, "Jack Cali", The once Lost Poet, of Hopes, Centric Rambles, giving furry to "The Pen name 'The 3rd Wright' of M." A "Future Art, of Knot's PO^2".

Jack Cali, the Calico Jack pirate of the tracks. With a cooO to Cats and Wolves of Sheep's yelling "baaaas" into mountain Goats. As a man, made friends with the beasts that hunted his herd, lost. And found man's best friend just wants some food and to smell the hillside. beside the path now singularly protected by multiple animals of cave and land. Coexisting exceptionally with new catch games & ...

"Smell that boy?! The rabbit is running through the hills to great us, at burrows a-top the same hills. From under the same tree of apples we rest, and thump a beat to our whistle, howling at the moon to announce simple. SOUL, FILLED JOY! Of thankful existence. And a sculpted gift of pure human gem. Given as the "Green Eyed Monkey Boy" fell from a tree to be a man, with a truly unique poetry of imaginative sand.

__A Man of Many Names__

A man of many names, is forever a feather falling. Into gravity's inevitable grasp. Never destined to fly again. While becoming part of the largest mass, flying through the time of space. A Never truly known perception, of an egg fried on an accident of winds.

Drum Rum Mold

Drum, Rum, Mold.
Dollars Lured Readily,
Into Existence of writing!
Box office delights.
"You infamous, Tree man."

You know you have to hear it from me to see the Speak "speak!" right in-front, of a dictionary of turnZ.

    Jack Cali, lost to the poetry of life's true Hope. Furiously Fated, to Educate one's own mind.
    While Dan so devilishly marked his way back home.
    As a monkey of a boy climbed out of sight, into the sky. To fly like a bomb to the ground. Bouncing on bent knees, leaving marks of cut time.

    Reflecting a mirrored mirage, from my blind Spot., evolving beyond the ancestor's howl at the moon.

Under the soul spinner, spirt sprinter, mind remarkably tamed relentlessly. "The Man of Many Names" first ever defined use, of "Po~LuReD" a genre, word, shift emulsified.
Emotional Tail of Stories stored, shelved into corners of globes, squarely, Pi-I-eyed.

While ingesting the color to never be rung, dry by suns light on an already cracked Liberty BeLieved to be Freely rippling, wrinkles into tortuous tortoise-Shellz holding, rabbit soup. For the cat to lap. To tease the monkey. Who forgot he was a boy, with the key to a plan of Eureka!

Snowballed onto beaches of freedom in life. To afford anything of value. Besides the molten golden Sun, and invaluable bright blue birds, song filled beaks, each uniquely carved like shells on a beach.

For spirits to whip through. Spiraling out faster than thought as whistled chirps so happy to flowers under the sun. Across the land of sparrows who befriended the gulls of the seas. Who remind me to simply say, thank you, to A Jem.

Not yet filled with SEe-As to tURn Sand into muddy bed rock. To grow in every entity, of minds soul filled colored sense of smell. Of emotionally butterflied eyes on spirits, you chime into existence. While learning your drips of mass, from energy expelled from starting your finish.

    A droplet once. Every century carving the river to crack open. Unleashing the demonic and angelic natures of balance. In a slow untamed eruption.
    Over billions, time counted to none. Instantly turned into a void of the prettiest of stars, planets. Giving gravity to orbit. Or-bit by bit, shift stardust across universes void, of frozen waves.

    Using currents, only learned by those with an eye to see the unseen. Learning adaptations, of boo! A little cloud of dust spins round in place, but orbits near three colors of old.
    Excess Red from your early millenniums.

A BURRRR OF ICE SHARDS BLUE IN SHAPE.
AND SOUND COMES RYTHMICLY OUT!
YELL-O!!!
A -ROUND-ABOUT!
    We need More Thumping, Bumping, Humping! But no trumping, new sight on primary geoids.
Because, bam!

Here is what happens when blue sand meets "YeLL-O!"
and! And there you see me, created in all the silence. As all gardens grow and die. Creating Dimond shells of fossil fueled black holes. Blindly shimmering all rays of energy in all forms of light.

Including a tree noticed briefly, as a red seed falls between the lines, of mortal mass and matter. And not quite in spiritually, soul soothed, existence place of worth.

As it passes the death defining sound of "Yell-O! It steals a pinch of RE-adD, existence. Creating an O-range Sun Rise.

Making me glade you can-not predict my manna, being a banana. For that monkey boy to eat & fall up the roots.

-The Man of many names.
-A Knotted Note

"Self-Destruction for Self-Preservation"
(Unedited)

Daniel Harkness
Introduction to Philosophy 100 01
02/18/11
Self Destruction for Self Preservation
[My Philosophy of Life] (then)

    During life, we live our lives in a monotonous, follow the leader. While most aspire to be the leader, few sit, pondering and watching the leader, in-order to not make the same mistakes as them. While remembering what they did well/right. The building block of human societies basis. But it is those who take the time to listen and learn, while being objective to any and every idea, that become the leaders through history and are the ones that we look to to carry us into the future.

    It is for this reason that I have always pushed myself to be my own worst critic, while holding a weight of infinite mass upon myself to be the so called "hero". I do not think of myself in anyway better then anyone, if I think of myself at all, it is below everyone else. And always remembering that there is something much greater then the small piece the human race plays in the idea of existence.

 I am always coming up with new theories off of my own experiences through my life. And trying to always figure out who I am, and my role in the present moment. It is because of this one theory I have lived by (out of many) Is "Self Destruction For Self Preservation".

 In order to understand being self destructive to preserve ones self we first need to understand what Self Destruction and Self Preservation really is. And how it can be used to further create an understanding of how to better preserve ourselves.

 Self Destruction can mean many different things, depending on the context. The general human context conceptualizes it as destructive acts, Self inflicted acts that are harmful physically, mentally, and emotionally. In another context it could be perceived as pulling apart your own self/personality. Such as putting yourself in bad situations, but in general destroying what makes you, You.

Now that we have an understanding of Self Destruction, what is self preservation? Self preservation can be viewed as; survival of an organism, the traits of emotions that keep organisms alive, such as pain, fear, happiness, hope, instinct to reproduce, for humans the entirety of the love to hate spectrum. The biases of self sufficient motives, and spreading to leaving your mark, and defining yourself as an individual.

Now with an understanding on Self Destruction and Self Preservation, how does self destruction allow for self preservation?

By breaking down who we are and pushing our own boundaries, we are able to figure out who we really are as a human, a being, a soul, something that exists, and further into how we see ourselves in the society around us. Along with how others see us. By understanding and finding who we are, we are then able to preserve the unique things that make us, US!

By making Destructive marks on our own selves, and lives; physically, mentally, emotionally, and metaphorically, we create our own personal life stories that we uniquely have and know. And then we are the only ones who can make the choice to share or keep to ourselves. By making these types of marks on our own personal lives we end up preserving the real us in an everlasting way in our own mind.

By physically being destructive to ourselves we create preservations of pieces of ourself through our own actions. That can either be lost in-time or forever preserved in time. Our self preservation inside our own mind and body can also be done through Writing, Art, Music, spoken word and actions. Any form of lasting can be considered an art. The broadest category humans are capable of perceiving when grouping things into categories.

For example; art has been considered as everything from the Mona Lisa, to a toilet. From Beethoven's "Ode to Joy" to a four hour silence that was preformed. Because music is not only sound but the absence of sound. And from a quote to a novel.

For me personally I have covered all Self Destructive acts not solely by random occurrence of my life. But also by purposely going out of my way to put myself in unneeded situations. By pushing myself to my limits physically, mentally, and emotionally.

I have done this through the jobs I have chosen, and decide to quite, how I have dealt with money, how I have made my own path through the education world, how I have slept for weeks (getting up only to eat and use the bathroom), kept myself up for days, pushed my self to walk for days on end even after I could no longer wear shoes due to blisters on my feet or bend my knees because of how swollen they where. All by a choice to push myself in the name of Love. I made the decision to live on the streets for two and a half months, when I was 19 starting when it would still be below 0 out. And after spending close to a year living in an apartment from the age of 18. There was no need for me to really do this. But I choose to. Because I would not leave my friend alone and on his own. And under the pretense of Love, but later found in myself something that I would of never found otherwise.

    I have always allowed myself to explore Artistically, Musically, in Literature, and My own mind. With a result of being so self destructive at points that I did not know if I would see the sunrise. But Preserving myself in my own mind in such a way that today, I know myself and limits so well that its as if I have prewritten my own life and the lives around me. But yet I am always surprised astonished and excited by something as simple as a new spin on an old thought.

    Taking ideas previously created by others an adopting them for our selves, is a truly unique human trait. And then by building our own ideas from breaking down others. And constantly adapting ourselves. By carrying our own genes on through our children, but yet having the ability to be so compassionate we will take on the task of adopting someone else's offspring and raising it as our own. How we affect our surroundings, Being the only animal that destroys to create. As if we are worthy of being gods.

Humans in general tend to think of ourselves as better/the smartest our of all the animals, that we barley even think of ourselves as animals. To the point where in some cases we think and hold ourselves as not being categorized in the animal group (when considering religion and where we stand in the pyramid of our standings between the bottom of the chain and god.

As humans we crave self preservation. It is truly one of our greatest and worst flaws. But by being self destructive I can only come to the final conclusion that it is done for self preservation. For example by destroying our own skin with tattoos we truly create the ultimate form of destroying our selves to create something, art.

Self Destruction and Self Preservation is truly one of my greatest theory pieces and ideas on how to live your life to the fullest. Among many other aspects of my past I know that by living my life with this as an idea in-ground in me for as long as I can remember.

Self-Preservation is something that all being strive for, in our own mind, or in the books of history. By in-order to do this along the way it is needed to be self-destructive at times. This is why I choose to live by this theory of Self Destruction for Self-Preservation.

Notes

•◇∞•◇∞•◇∞•◇∞•◇∞•◇∞•◇∞

›Mark‹

_/_/_ ©™® _/_/_

Beer After Beer

Beer after Beer.
Smoke a Cigarette,
Wonder...
Wonder, Why?

Why have things gone.
The way they have?

I miss when I was.
Loved by everyone.
That time is gone.
Past.

What has happened to the past?
Lost to the present.

So many friends, I had.
So many friends, lost.

Money?
Jobs?
Drugs?

Pick one

Your choice.
It's one of the three.
light, inhale.

What am I doing?
the same Thing over and over Again?

What am I doing?
What choice do I have?

I scream but no-one hears.
I scream for a dream.

This world is crashing down.
Down.
Down.

Down to the towns
around me.

Our dreams.
Come crashing down.
Around our lives.
Till we are too old to care.
Why?

Why is nothing possible anymore?
What's that knock at the door?

Death?
XXX
Three
The number of me.
The balance.

I am falling, someone catch me.
The balance, will fall with me.
I know of one.
Who can save me?

But they are lost.

When we fall,
So will you.
Our deaths will be the end.
They have given up.
I am about to.
Will we stop this?
Do we want to?

Like a nightmare from my past.
I know what will happen.
The end is near.
For our souls, are giving up.
The gods are falling.

I want to tell everyone the truth.
But deaf ears are all around.
How to speak the truth.
Time grows silent
Do you hear it?
I don't

I am waiting for a noise.
Sounding the start of a new.
Before there is no sense,
left to use.

I sang when I was young
I whistled when I was a teen
I whistled
I am silent
Now, I am silent
I try
I am trying
To create sound

-Hope
-The Lost poet
Age 21

Notes

•◇∞•◇∞•◇∞•◇∞•◇∞•◇∞•◇∞

_____

›Mark‹

_ _ _ / _ / _ ©™® _ / _ / _ _ _

•◇∞•◇∞•◇∞•◇∞•◇∞•◇∞•◇∞•◇∞•◇∞•◇∞•◇∞•◇∞•◇∞•◇∞•

A Great Man (A Teacher)

A Great Man.

A Great!

I Knew.

I knew a Great!

Knowing is what, man has called, one of the greatest achievements.

But history has shown us, knowing is our greatest accomplishment.

The simple achievements of men, can be summed up into two categories.

The knowledge we know from discovering. And the Knowledge we pass on.

My Grandfather endlessly discovered knowledge, while passing it on to those who wanted to listen.

I never had to read any of his works to understand this. But I did need to take the time to listen.

A great man, a lost relic of information now. He always wanted those around him to grow from the experiences he had discovered. It might have been in stories.

It might have been a simple author he loved. Like a human library, he just wanted everyone to grow and learn. It wasn't about the time or money. It was about the stories, passed down.

A great man is not one of wealth. Not one of class, Knowledge. A great man is someone who wants nothing but to better those they come in-contact with.

If I recall the last project Donald (My Grandfather) was working on. Was one to remember a relative's life. He might have had an endlessly boring way of describing this. But don't all the Harkness'. The point being. Who tries to remember someone anymore, with a manuscript to their life? Very few. The internet we all hope will convey this in a way.

I myself have been working on a book {not this one} for countless years. One in which I hoped Donald (My Grandfather) would read. And now in memory need to finish.

But I feel the best way to remember this great man.

As if we all wrote a single page about a man, so great that they are memorable enough to not wait for someone who didn't know him, to write his book.

To write it as a collective. I unfortunately know so little of this man's life. And would enjoy to one day hold a cup of tea while reading about him, as I look out at life, I am so thankful to have. Only because my father and mother where able to give me a life I could appreciate, because of those who raised them.

-Daniel Timothy Harkness

Into A Box of Living Dreams

Mmmmm, breath in, whistle.
And out it comes from the shadows of my lungs.
A voice stuck in everyone's mind.
Begins a-new, From the box of living dreams.
Trapped within Me.
Drowning in pain, as a laugh rolls out.

I try to let it flow like raindrops, falling down.
I try to sing what I mean, as the shy guy.
Choking me with a tricky trap of foul bones.
Reminding a body of sung hums. With breaths of orgasms.

Of padded down sound. Into weathered sand.
Shimer and shake the new wave, through bodies now.
Vibrating vocal cords, like electric vibrations.
Echo loud in rhythm of hearts so hurt.

They forgot, with another is to rebuild the gap of broken past.

Your spirit begins to fool your soul. As I mind your heart.
Counting each beat with great mind.
To shock the repetition in you.

Restarting a new.
Suddenly I hit the beat, like wind through wheat.
I sow a new seed, a live, flowing through the trees.
I suddenly see, a reason to sleep.
To dream.

I Pulled the rhythm out of my mind.
Setting it to the side.
A decade in waiting.
Watching your minds baking.

Melting down, my own mind.
Into a golden nugget of selected sound.
Rhythmically taking... All in, the making.

__Notes__

•◇∞•◇∞•◇∞•◇∞•◇∞•◇∞•◇∞

_____

›Mark‹

__/_/_ ©™® _/_/_

•◇∞•◇∞•◇∞•◇∞•◇∞•◇∞•◇∞•◇∞•◇∞•◇∞•◇∞•◇∞•◇∞•

The Information Given

Maybe we can trick a treat of twelve candied dirty fruit, times on hallowed eves. But you have to do you.

But also, commonly brought to picnics in the coming of America you gave me a Yosemite of history, I wish the schools highlighted in more of an adventure of, let's go see these great things everyone. A foundation of learning. Would be the rain catcher to gutters. To purify, that rain and give a man some work, when he is able and sane. With grounds that sit broken down for no reason but profit.

Assign a manager of construction to a daily made crew of, who woke up that day and could and willing to give an hour or a few.

All that change in time. To mend the fences
and learn the fields. To just walk around finding old trees of species not from that wood. A poisonous thing if not rooted out. But those bugs purpose, I'm sure, of ecological sense can find a home, to bug beetle to their hearts... do they? They must in exoskeleton growth.

Could you imagine! That being tomorrow's suit- fashion, left on Madison and used by those unfortunately needing shelter... no more the beetles would say. Give them a room at the old factory and see what help he can give back in their way.

Maybe just by being an ear for a rambler to find an end to that days, sentence of memorable thoughts. Birds like to sing along. With "he-he" bells of beetles. On wires of man. These animals... Events are truly, truly grand to watch run- about. In self-made feathers while theirs are stuck on our heads. Now that's some news Red. Oh your right Mr blue Jay. One day the sparrows across the pond might even sing the same song. After we set the tone for the symphony of earthly equal grown. A ballet. To be danced for all. In a written Wright of creative thought. BTW who said I am to be called by the name red bird and you by blue. I prefer ivy for my tweets grew and grew around old oaks that my home of ancestors past laid farmers sheep threads. Of last sheerings for fashion is Mary's this year. And singing a sigh-lent spot light piece. That odd bahhh sheep.. wait, that's a mountain goat! Oh words a lovely miracle-growing crafts.

Say hi to a tree today or flower and I'll do the same.

The Only Imposter

I corrupted myself. So, I could find Love.
I stopped time. So, love would remember me.
I called my decay. Before my heart exploded.

Anchoring my soul. While my spirit flew.
Picking Tulips off, at the knees.
A box of simple sound.
I am the pronounced.

I fell from the trees,
The playsets.
In a mind
I am the COME. back. KID.

The Kid. Who Came Back.
That Kid who gave to life.
To the Impossible.
Death becomes You
I Am, the only Imposter.

      -The only Original.

      -The Lost Poet

__Notes__

•◊∞•◊∞•◊∞•◊∞•◊∞•◊∞•◊∞

_____

›Mark‹

_ _/_/_ ©™® _/_/_

•◊∞•◊∞•◊∞•◊∞•◊∞•◊∞•◊∞•◊∞•◊∞•◊∞•◊∞•

A Beginning of Muddy Tracks

The shelves of "sighhh"...-lent peace.

A moving relic of all needed furniture, of a single partition. And a hopeful dining table of pieces to be given to the cousins and grandkids as names dates, symbols rest on an event of dinning. Only able to have, when all the pieces together. With new shelves of yearly journals, stacked thoughts, of life to begin and end again. and again. Forever my friends.

At an old home, I found an interesting set of shelves. The first one I moved dropped an unsettling peace of an old book.

Pg.226 revelations XXL
And it first reads
(on one side)

"The river of the water of life. To The tree of life."

I have been feeling a very unsettling attachment to existence.

I am now sitting back in a place. That

something first started. A writing. Along with a challenge for myself.

As I was in a way trying to find reason, in how I perceived the world around me. Only in a way, to better understand myself. While creating a thrill-ing brand new piece of art.

As it seemed the whole world was going through an extreme change.

I found myself finally defeated, but still trying to see the beauty in finally becoming me.

I wrote a paper (The Silhouette of Time), in response to someone I met. They gave me a link to a few videos. Explaining a personality type, I felt always partial to. But not exactly the same. A seventeenth personality type if you will.

I concluded to myself I am none of the understood but a mix between the last two. Perspective and introverted. How alone I felt. But even the loneliest of things has a purpose.

And it was time for me to allow something I've always known, So I could find my purpose. Finally finishing the projects, I have been doing small pieces for almost 16 years.

I had to first sort the jumble of my life, along with understanding there is no one who can or will tell me how to be.

All things living and absent. Really are a constant construct of molecular events of being.

A friend reminded me of one of my old sayings. "The Only Original!". But everyone perceives this at first as a narcissistic thing to say. (Meaning I strive for originality, and we are all unique and there for original).

I took an extremely difficult diagnosis, given when I was younger. But learned to understand I was not. I was always trying to explain how I feel. But to positively be. Or fight extreme depression and manic things of emotional and physical pain.

I learned slowly how to control myself. Anger was the first. I started to take a deep breath. And try to see another path to a discussion.

Logically thinking this is not the right time or option.

The endless control others seem to want. When all I want is control of my being, myself, My thoughts, My mind, My heart.

I have always felt Judged and after a period of time. You stop caring what others think, "per say". For the opinion of someone is an absolute human condition. I sometimes forgot to acknowledge, for being so used to having my own-self, judging every step I take.

As if even solid rock was almost soft and fragile. A self-taught pressure to never step on a crack, and avoid leaving a trail. Unless it was meant to be, so that the journey of a safe travel can be followed.

I always found awe in the world around me, with a wonder of why simple things where never as special to everyone else.

For even the mark of ink on my back was made as a slight joke. But also made to be an almost shirt tag. As if I came off an assembly line. A Reward to myself after accomplishing, a task of trying to with-stain from drinking for just two weeks (A goal completed by going a full month).

The Tattoo, made to be read by those above. For I feel there is always a higher power.
And it reads:
> "If the Gods are watching,
> We might as well put on a good show".

I've been growing my Art With wonder. I realized my existence is just that. A big art production of a creative mind. Swimming in the depths, of this awkward confusing human existence.

While I consider myself extremely lucky. I struggle to remember that, I am loved and truly blessed. While remembering to Honor and Respect myself.

Given not just one, but multiple sets of parents and people to admire.

The funny thing is the more I live the more that I find.

An "American" born. In the area of New York {Valhalla} . Grown, with summers in the New England suns, sea breeze. An Amazing self-built family. With culture of every kind. And the ability to watch everyone else grow ahead of me. Being the youngest.

An Idea, or better yet IDEA(R). For what fun I thought it'd be to not only write a book of originality. But create new words and definitions to be understood. For an "Idea??" Is to me an upswing in notation that is more of a hypothesis.

"I have an "ideaahhhh" help me find the conclusion.

I have an ideaR " an already well thought out plan. Help me construct it. This type of thinking goes on, to how one of the books I have been working on, but had to change the title.

So, I tried my best to withhold the new title. But sometimes I couldn't help but tell, in Excitement! Because it is exciting to me whenever I figure out the end solution, to a thought in my mind. That "ah Ha!" moment.

The saddest part of the literary journey has been. my own grandfather, I found out after he passed, I should have asked for guidance.

He never heard a single writing of mine.

While the second time I ever read to a crowed. Was a note, a poem of sorts writing to my father. For I could only convey my sorrow and simply, emotions of his loss through writing "A Great man".

So "CoLuRounds of a Cook."© will be the second book I publish.

The never-ending process of maddening amounts of papers of rambles. And well thought out writings.

I Taught myself to see not, a run-on sentence, but a subject matter. while normally very confused with how the grammar aspect should be. As I am sure, it is noticeable.

I taught myself to depict the notion into the thought. Into the "ideaR" of a picture of a understood rhythm of persevered and understood colored sense.

This is Called a "Po~LuRed": A piece of creation that is a genre all its own. Shifting and emulsifying emotion with physical and spiritual sense of material and immaterial mass. Constructive in geometric forms of sense.

So, I worked on three aspects of how I would become a self-sustained man into my Thirties.

Spending my "Twen-teens", as an almost extended who, what and what's, that?! Of so much Sun & fun! But 30 I'll go into the actual work. Putting the puzzle together I had to keep strewn across my existence.

Delayed Greatly by events, the world struggled through, along with personal, and direct attempts at stopping my progression.

I can barely remember something without putting it or creating an almost click of locking it in place. Others took advantage of this, changing or distracting my plans to work on different aspects. I remember what, ought to, where without thinking of the actual original data, of my brains "broken bits". I somehow glued back together with the hope of a song in my heart, a whistle on my lips and all the tasty colorful creations... I always think of, three or more ways to improve and just make B!-E!-A!-U!-ti-FUL!

From the taste and smell. Of the "Recipe Book" to the sculpting of a "Poetry Book".

Now this thought structure, you would think is enough for one book, But no. It had to be the three-part understanding of ABC, musically with a fun-tail, or "Lur" of storybook kind of fun. That only started a whole new journey of learning!

"A true book of beauty. Why? Because why not! Ya, know what.. Make it Two, maybe 3 endlessly."

While needing to create a way to break through my struggle.

Working towards a dream, built off a question, Asked by my second father of sorts. What is your ultimate dream?

At thirteen I replied "to buy back my old house". For that is my idea of Perfection. Rolling gardens, a pool and old stone BBQ to giving way to amazing gatherings of friends and family.

While the old studio would be an open floor plan, of a guest room and a second kitchen. To entertain and maybe even make my now unstoppable, snowball of full planned thought of a really immersive reality.

Umbrellaed under a fun play an ode to my Dog. It would be called "Cali-Co" you see. While the catering company of "Dan Good Products" & "Butler Hill Catering" is some of the other branched businesses of thought. Giving way to now solid plans to pursue All forms of products, media, and General interests.

To all of a sudden be seen by my old friends and family who always endured my endless curiosity of infinite rooted IdeaRs.

But never completed redundantly because I would realize just how to make it, even drip this delicious decision of fully experienced me. "CHEF daddy" "The Dancing Chef" once (upon a time) as they first called me in the kitchen of "Lava". A whole new book for another time.

But "Dan good products" has to come with a start of sauce "Sassy Sauces" Company to dip as you read, and cook and talk. With these IdeaRs of already put together but separated business plans. I release them all at once with a podcast, an extra treat.

But now done with a poetry book release.
as a preview, and marketing addition.
A board is instant you see..?

And to add the best of fun for that is the way I view work... as fun games of "oooo, let me let me!"

But never allowed to let myself/"that monkey boy" of daring to dangle from the tops of trees.

I say I have a release, of all these almost fully complete. And what about a quick series that is me experiencing a travel across the county. To enjoy in a light of Gay intensity. Call it by the fun game it'll be. "The great Grind". For I will see the fun places of the night clubs recommend to me.

While the actual amazing culture of be who you want to be. We all are modified beasts of choose your animal, your sound. "Unleash the Zoo!"

As Sundays are spent exploring the brunch spots. Of hungover "mans day of rest" before the week.

With showing at all the best boutiques. But having a game of if your see the Gay of the day you get a card and pass to have some coffee with me at the house, I built from dreams of 1,2,.1,2.,1,2. Three. A growing thought, like a tree of an amazing good company with an endless system of possibilities. Unfurling an Art of "Noted Knots".

With oh yes! "Sassy Sauce Talk" in the end. With "Sughar Dan-dee" the drag star of messy sunflower dresses. Never brought to light, incorporating all this.

In act one of little old me, has been thinking this up while baking in the sun. Frozen with fear of failing if not started in that year. The 20s are back and I'm the brand. The modern 20s Man. A PO2. For no one wanted to, play my games, of actual build this with me. The following week of the best trick or treat, holiday, island hopping fun.

So, I had to learn it'll have to be me. Paving a new path to a new idea. To just the most, creative centric hum, unheard, great new bird of beauty.

Giving all while surprises, of this event of a man coming out of left field. Like a good old grand slam. A sad note, sometimes. But help is the power of my family and friends. To polishing the manual of the soon to be endlessly offered. And the investments of need-be. To fulfill this dream.

But through something I kept deep inside me. A golden light of positive negative balance. How I make it through the darkest of times.

And still climb to see, the top of the mountains. Always the last to see the suns glory, over Great worldly gifts of Gia and that salty father sea. I cannot just jump the rope of Jack's cracks. But sell the colorful dream, worried with blinding love. That is best written, not so jumbled placement seen.

So, the stage of the products the dried pasta was dated on my way back from Miami. For I make dreams and run as hair, with tortious shell, learned capability. Only learned because I took the time to find, my finesse in being a fish of the twelve-star sign.

Decoding an immersive life rhyme. I wrote into a cat's-tail, to jog my memory. When it was needed and only made with pure intentions, of wanting to be amazing.

With all the greats before me. I humbly wrote a letter of my family are like a real melting pot of American "Hall of Famers". Unfortunately lost.

Each in their own right of business, sports, mothers, fathers, artists, teachers and really just good old Boyz of Boston, Italian. With N.Y. in ground from the other side. and unintended, assembled longest of isles of the new Amsterdam of York bound.

For the rummers were started as an untruthful hunt on a broken man. Trying to understand who he was, while getting to know the past family through helping to sell a homestead, that I cherished.

It sheltered me from the storm, of the most iconic self-destruction for self-preservation. Not ready to be seen. But treated as some joke to, pick at him until he cracks. Or leaves.

For comments made were not very neighborly. And I in no way would ever do the things you made assumptions and twisted stories. For someone who was trying to replant their true self of a self-made man of some already odd tendencies.

For teaching what I learn is the biggest delight for me. And no hard feelings but maybe say hi, and talk to me. I'd explain how the questions were never asked directly.

A side note: A new gay support group should really be made. For its all vicious in ways, most do not even understand or see.

While my heart stayed strong with finishing my Book in the summer of 2020 (unfortunately this was not accomplished).

And finding a specific poetry no longer lost to the Black-Cat (Midnight) of a jazzy downtown beat. But belonged and shown with a pure thought, cotton tailed rabbit. Who even struggled with the chapters of white and black, placement being a concern, perceived.

For we are all equal and have our own tastes of delicious capacity. The gardens are no longer just for the snake and an evolution of broken ribs you see. It's for all the creatures and beings of past - present- future.

All told from a man who gave names, to the times he saw as his own right of creative minds sight. A big challenge only done with specifics, given to that rabbit named cat. That man of writing the one they call Dan, Danny, Tan-Dan, The Hark-2-the-ness. That monkey boy, of curiosity. Climbing the tallest trees, to watch his own family play wiffle ball, bache, and eat all the taffy. After working hard through New England winters.

A family of all adopted kids, cousins. With family stemming from, Brooklyn old. Boston farmers-markets, the departed beds were made by American grit.

Hoping to accomplish my own.

For even though cruel. At the end of an unfortunately long battle, that many are also dealing with. In this very uncomfortable and untaught, but money bidding and forwardly, seems to be a witch hunt.

That for me has been destroying a life's work.

You were just too curious to wait and see. And give a creationist their privacy. So, like a caged animal with only, their mind to sound back reverbs. Of what was that? The house or someone trying to break-in let me, see?! I smelled the body spray of someone at one point.

So don't pretend I'm the only one doing things out of the bounds of normal. I just almost lost myself completely to a plan hatched by someone for what reason?!

Because of fear of just asking me? Who I was or why I am me?! Explaining myself, one day at a time.

So, my soul can finally, hopefully, find a loving peace. Before I move on to my own theory's, I've sculpted.

Because that is what existing is. Finding the path that you are meant to slip, fall, and wake up.

As a time, honored, a call out on the 4th hear comes Me! And did my count of fireworks over a providence bridge beautify. My art is here!

With this being a partial letter of seeking investors? Help me make this reality so I can start a process of tasteful travel. An open Playlist of what do you like? And did you see! That sunset Oh! the beauty!

A side note. Anyone well known for any

reason leave them be. Let them live normally. Congratulate them at the appropriate areas of events galleries, concerts, when they are working. For A few of them I can see just want to be free living like you and the "American dream".

But I digress, along an almost rolodex of ideas to be explored, ideaRs to be made/done. And me seeing an end dream. Ending as a retired old man, with a shack, that tequila and rum drinks, kabobs or w/e is just freely made when my tired old self of a man" isn't floating in the ocean or playing with the sand.

A vague image of bits of the pieces I have been sculpting in an artist heart.

Thank you, this is the man of many names. But Daniel Timothy Harkness, I am happy to say I came back to a note of an old whistle heard round. A start to a beginning, of a new.

> We are all in it together with the stairs on our horizon of new depths of history untold.

I Have the Perfect Curse.

I HAVE THE PERFECT CURSE.

I HAVE THE ABILITY TO CREATE A RIPPLE OF SOUND.

THOUGHT IS THE LEADER, OF FOLLOWERS.

A CONCISE DEPICTION OF UNDERSTANDING THE COMPREHENSIVE EXISTENCE.

THE PERCEIVED NOTION OF A TIME FRAME.

A DEFINITION PROVING EXISTENCE OF A MOMENT.

INSTANTLY BECOMES HISTORY.

TRYING TO PREDICT A FUTURE.

WHICH IS A SPACE BEHIND THE PAST AND PARALLEL TO THE INEVITABLE CONVERGENCE OF THE BEGINNING AND END OF A SINGLE IDEA OF THOUGHT.

UNDERSTANDING THIS, A TESSERACT BECOMES A REALITY OF OUTSIDE THE BOX THINKING, AFFECT OF INFINITE DIRECTIONS.

EACH WITH A PATH TO THE SIGHT OF SOUNDING-OUT OUR OWN COLOR OF SENSE.

KNOWING HOW OUR OWN EXISTENCE IS FED INTO OUR MIND, HEART AND SOUL.

A SINGLE NOTION, IS A COMBINATION OF SENSES PERCEIVED BY THE NONEXISTENT PRESENT FORM, FROM PAST TO PRESENT OF DEFINED LAYERING OF A PREVIOUSLY CREATED IDEA. AN IDEA THAT ONLY EXISTS DUE TO SELF AWARENESS OF ONE SOURCE OF MATTER CREATED BY THE ENERGY OF TWO OPPOSITELY CHARGED EFFECTS.

ACTIONS ARE AS SIMPLE AS A WORD IN THE MIND, A COLOR TO THE EYE, A SOUND IN THE EAR, TOUCHING THE DELICIOUS TAST OF LIFE. BEGINNING THE COMPLETE THOUGHT OF DEATH, A BEING/BEGINING THE ANSWERS IN-ORDER TO GIVE INSTRUCTION ON HOW TO MANIPULATE A SINGLE ENTITIES OWN CHOICE OF DIRECTION.

THIS RIPPLE WILL BE HEARD ACROSS ALL COLORS OF MASS. TO SET ALL ON THEIR OWN UNIQUE PATH TO THE BEGINNING OF FINAL TRUTH. A WISDOM FOUND IN THE ABSENCE OF THE DARKEST AREA OF LIGHT.

THIS DECISION OF AN IDEA, WAS CREATED. IN A FORM OF A BET. TO SEE IF THIS NOTION WOULD BE FORGOTTEN OR REMEMBERED BY THOSE WHO CALL THEMSELVES WORTHY OF MEMORY AND THOUGHT. WHICH STARTED THE FIRST RIPPLE OF LOVE & HATE, FATE & HOPE, PAIN & PLEASURE, CHARITY & GREED.

THE PRIZE OF THE BET...? FINAL PEACE OF THE INFINITE TORTURE OF BEING THE FIRST TO LAST

I WILL NEVER REMEMBER TO FORGET

~ Dan (Written at 16)

Fates hope is to succeed at the game of life. a strategy of pains undying love, to be wrong about the lye of existing in a perfect & permanent balance with its best friend and gift death.
~ Centric ›(Written at 16)

Icy Glass of Dawns Break

Icey glass of dawns break, giving future promises of blooming farms, delicious foods of unknown colorful combinations. Dancing flavors across tongues watering the growth of new harvests.

Waiting to be shattered like the thin mirror of frozen molecules across the ponds and lakes. Begging to be shattered by the impossibly hard boulders yearning to be thrown by the destructive inner child. To disrupt the peaceful calm. As the warm light rises. Changing the grounds, within what we perceive as, a short 1/24th of a trip around the golden danger. Unknown to all but the commanding hand of an unproven entity pulling the strings behind the great curtain of spatial universe known.

Surrounding the world, we call home. With little thought to how the beauty briefly experienced by a lucky default. Being a lucky conciseness in this mishap of what we call life. Will soon break the cold of seasons. Giving spring the greenest eyes, of a child born under two fish, signed in the stars. Who strives to break the bounds of the human goals?

Creating a path that throws not just land on a map. But the sound of cracking ice melting the greys of winters pass with a vocabulary complex, created communication, thought to be derived from human consciousness. Not the vibrations clicking the time between cells. Splitting to create the infinite sands of time.

As the dead leftovers of our physical forms create the infinite stardust. That is pulled toward each-other, small at first. But creating the masses we call soil. And as friction creates the spark that ignites, the most active into new centers of solar systems.

Taking on personalities of baby gods choosing their paths into the dark cold of endless space. Using tools made of their own creation, to navigate compasses of flat appearance. But truly understood is a tesseract of infinite navigation.

That uses the true key keepers, to know how to split themselves, so each spirt, soul, heart, mind, takes a post to sail around broken attempts of dead eggs, only to further the existence by the choices made by the suns pull on the living and death balance, that is not taught.

But self-learned as a simple chess game of infinite colors, tastes, smells, sights, touch, sounds, wrapped in endless energy warming and cooling a pendulum of precise balance.

Science has tried to ask and explain.
Religion has created stories of hope and fear.

Keeping the masses from wondering the truth. Known across history. As the scary fact that god is but a child passing through lives of stars maps.

Growing, evolving, learning. As time lapse to the bitter end of all the past suns, that glitter our nights. To a simple end of learning how to shape and further existence. For their own selfishness. Or to sacrifice for the other baby souls looking for spirits. To help them learn there sparks, to warm the skies with their own, colors of unknown future hues.

-Dan

-Jack Cali

-PO^2

Notes

•◇∞•◇∞•◇∞•◇∞•◇∞•◇∞•◇∞

———————————————————————————

›Mark‹

_/_/_ ©™® _/_/_

•◇∞•◇∞•◇∞•◇∞•◇∞•◇∞•◇∞•◇∞•◇∞•◇∞•◇∞•◇∞•

The MiMi© of Tim€

The MiMi© of time is the cell shift I devoted myself to study, the first "Guinea Pig" of knowingly separated time. The one who learned to store memories, secrets, and abilities, through a multi3 singular2 l1ne. Of existing mass within themselves. Consisting of Past Present and Future forms.

Being able to switch in endless directions, changing the pattern of time, but still able to find the symbols of "round sound". That help to mold an energy of flat line into a seed of time. Planting it, with rhythmic rhymes, that place, the beginning @ the center, of all time.

Using intricate webs made of Co-Lur-fulL molecular explosions. $pitting out a reverb of what is to come now.

From the future of history read, with a CaTching end that is DanƆed back into the ground with stomps and steps to process a numerical pattern back in sound. To the ending specific only to that string, the strand. pulled back upon, on the future tail end. So past and present flip, the rope of twisted present seeming to be a mortal dance all around the chalk lines on the ground. Stirring up a funny mixture of matter making up a cloud of a newly co1urfulL Jump Rope GAME.

An evolutionary speak whispered to past and present as matter twists around the future sound. So, all you see is a body just like you. Spinning a web of go-odly dreams with no preserved effect on anything said. But remember there is α co1urfulL MiMi© Of the Past & Present, pulling the strings of FUTURES PAST. The NEWest Fish to CATϽⅱ while feeling the tone of the Grand $lam, the CRACK of the Bat, into the true unknown. Another universe already filling with tricks to the building blocks, the real true switch. The worlds already lived and spun in matter into a kNew form of gold.

The actual soul is shaped! Each built from blocks of old that were pulled apart from each spirt held. The kNewEst speak from the Jacks creation. Is a LITERATION! On the brain path, whipping the sound of the pronounced. Off the sheet, it was written. Matter flowing through the hands, sculpting past lines wiped off the page into the future.

Showing sparks of new paths. A ricochet between the new gifts of gold & blue. While mistakes are a given, more than in a second determining, if its right? to think in patterns.

Scrapping whole worlds of infinite time, back down into a simple sounding rhyme. Known, threw one ear as BlU3, While MiMi©s in ¥our mind Thoughts of Gr€€n and you produce, a Sound Of Yel!oW. Through YoU and out into time.

Like sewing a new stitch into matter, to heal the rips, of the cracks growing. Shattering into the sand of times present / past we sweep them up and put them back into a glorious path of endless repercussions, to lead energy into the past. Viewed in your present eye connected to the mind, an almost computer chip, data bank, constantly being refined. Using past methods of trial and error.

I am the true terror, a mortal with a mind untold. Rewriting the stories of old with future tense and past being.

I switch the synapse before they start bleeding, A Sir-cut-Break. Breaking down the path, while spitting back a true delight, so the achieved path is redundantly done.

Etching a path into the bedrock for future paths to follow. Feeding the beast, I first created with a spark from a splinter dipped in sulfur, struck.

Against ridges of bones showing along the oldest of paths.

    The shock, the aww, that boom, that made the collide. The Cut, The Slit, The Rip, Into an Unknown. The universe, was once grown!

    So... I broke it down and made it mine. After telling you to look in my eye. A center of dark endless sound came out. Honing it down to the lips that you smack, and the credit I give right back. I used the knowledge known to make the bridges to futures past and jumped like a Rabbit.

    I cooed songs of Malic Birds. While I swayed as the Coo1estCat, coming down to listen to the g0Dly sound of a first recorded Snap-back. Of the Poet 1ost in his own sPace.

    Because an eXc3ntriᴐ man made a Ⱨop€ful thought at expanding outside the form of thought. To the body as an expansion slot. Making the space around, feel like nerves I've just first learned to touch.

    Expanding with each breath, in rolls through shapes of co1urle$$ told gold. A maTTe®

kind of speak, that suns explode to try and reach. While humans have right now the written speech, a tool. An endless loop of left over past.

Turned into the glass of a windows perspective, of the sands of time that I have to melt. In order to create its own time, its own Fucking mind!

The more it breaks, the better the crack, in the abyss. Of the yet unknown universe now.

That uses these parts and tools, in perfect harmonizing sound but seen only as a symbol, to unlock a riddle in the mind. To release the cell of endless time. Split it in two and tie a rope to each side. Spinning a gravitational force, of simple games of Tic Tac t0e. To teach my s0ul & spirit.

To mind my HeART & MiNd. But don't forget to find α Piece of TrEAsur3. And Your way back home. ¥our cosmic g0ld may predict the futures past.

That ends with a little, clap.

Very profound.

Notes

•◇∞•◇∞•◇∞•◇∞•◇∞•◇∞•◇∞

———————————————————————————

›Mark‹

_/_/_ ©™® _/_/_

•◇∞•◇∞•◇∞•◇∞•◇∞•◇∞•◇∞•◇∞•◇∞•◇∞•◇∞•◇∞•

0X0 The Mimic 0X0

The mimic of time is the cell shift I devoted myself to study the first Guinea-pig of separated time. The one who learned to hide memories, secrets, and abilities, through a multi singular line.

Being able to switch in endless directions, changing the pattern of time but still able to find. The symbols of "Round Sound" that helps to mold the energy, of that flat line into a seed of time. Planting it with rhythmic rhymes that place me at the beginning center of all time.

Using intricate webs made of colorful molecular explosions I spit out a reverb. Of what is to come now. From the future of history read, with a catching end that I dance back into the ground.

With stomps and steps to process a numerical pattern back in sound, to the ending specific only to that string. That strand. I pull back up on the future end. So past and present flip the rope of my present, seeming to be a mortal of ground dancing all around a funny mixture of matter and my own, made-up-sound.

An evolutionary speak! I whisper to past and present as I twist matter round the future sound. So, all you see is a body just like you, spinning a web of godly dreams. With no real effect on anything said.

But remember I'm saying the catch while feeling the tone of the grand-slam into the true unknown. Another universe I'm already filling with tricks, to the blocks of the real true switch.

The worlds you know I've already lived. And spun its matter into a k-new form of gold. The actual soul! Each built from blocks of old pulled from each spirt told.

The newest speak from Jacks creation, is a Literation! on the brain path, to wipe the sound of the pronounced, off the sheet its written. Into matter flowing into my hands. Sculpting past lines I whip, into the future. Showing sparks of new paths. A ricochet between the two I give gifts of gold and blue.

While mistakes are only human. More than in a second determining if its right, to think in patterns?

Scrapping whole worlds of infinite time, back down into a simple sounding rhyme. That I throw through your ear and out of time. Like sewing a new stitch, to heal the rips of the cracks growing. Shattering into the sand of times present and past.

I sweep them up and put them back, into a glorious path of endless repercussions, to lead energy into the past. While viewed in your present eye. The mind, a chip I constantly refine. Using past methods of trial and error.

I am the true terror, a mortal with a mind untold. Rewriting the stories of old with future tense and past being. I switch the synapse, before they start bleeding. Breaking down the path of light while spitting back a true delight.

Feeding the beast, I first created with a spark of endless rating. The shock. The AWW! That BOOM! That made the collide.

The cut, the slit, the rip, into the unknown!

The universe was once GROWN! So, I broke it down and made it mine.

After telling you to look in my eye. A center of dark endless sound came out. Honing it down to the lips that you smack. And the credit I give right back. I used the knowledge known to make the bridges to futures past and jumped like a bunny rabbit.

I cooed the song of birds. While all thought the coolest cat had just come down, to listen to the godly sound. Of a first recorded snap-back. Of the poet lost, in his own space. Because a centric man made a hopeful thought at expanding outside the form of thought, to the body as an expansion slot.

Making the space around like nerves I've just first learned to touch. Expand and breath, like a lung, in rolls through shapes of colorless told gold. A matter kind of speak! That suns exploded, to try and reach.

While humans got right now, the written speech. An endless loop of left over past. Turned into the glass of a windows perspective. Of the sands of time, that have to melt. To create its own fucking mind! The more it breaks the better the crack in the abyss, the black. Of the yet unknown universe now.

I'll use these parts, in perfect harmonizing sound, but seen only as a symbol. To unlock a riddle in my mind. To release the cell of endless time.

Split it in two, and tie a rope to each side, spinning a gravitational force of simple games of tic, tac, toe. To teach my soul and spirit. To mind my heart and mind. But don't forget to find your treasure. And your way back home. Your cosmic gold predicts the future.

That ends with a little clap.

Very profound.

-The Lost Poet

-Jack Cali

-The Artist Knot

The Sounding Sun

The sounding sun simply liberates the days, from unseen beauty.

As bricks of knowledge barricade classes from teaching worldly foundations of equally scripted language.   Squared in gardens of stone. We hoarded secrets of self-destructive progression as flaws of singularly originals, are shunned from the Heard echo of the cliffs.

Noting Knots of oaks silently falling, to new grounds of time-tested strength. Easily rotted by a generation of wooded pecks of soft feathered flight.

For the worm in the apple still decomposes the decomposition, of the oldest of Readily red cracks of giants, torn down for a shelter of excess. To simply reside just as hallowed in a lone state, of self-isolation.

Forgetting the unity of tribal songs. Around trees of man-made stars, on grounds alive with unimaginable existence. A grand garden of rounded ship. Through the unknown cold star-soaked blanket of expanding sound.

Colliding the ripples of a united existence is a needed flight of fancy. Whipping wonderful tides of new pools crafted along neighbors meeting yards. Fenced by only the games of skill to better the days of growth.

Brick and mortar, is not free. Without a foundation of motored movements of considerate compromises so neighborhoods, are city's yet lifted into the startling beauty, bestowed to all in sterling spotted nights.

With an Eden of delicious Gia green guidance. Seasoned with salty rough sanding seas. A simply smooth sounding path to suns of 7th generation plans. To echo the sound, as one.

A thanks to Sun and Stars, gifts of life.

Sound, sounds of sunny seconds, of precious games of hide and nightly seek. Oh, that Sun.

BOO TO THE MOON! THAT TIDE RISING COUSIN, OF PLUTOS CRACKER-JACK-CHEERS!

The meaningless glare of Sandys shells.

Absolutely tongue twisting, a rhythmic rhyme deep in the island palms fan.

A book, a meal, and a dream. Drumming back emulations, of beaches yet to be known by moon lit walks.
"Wonder why waterfalls worrI.E.?"
"Well. We wouldn't, wave wants to willing worlds, woven with wonderous wonders."

Notes

•◊∞•◊∞•◊∞•◊∞•◊∞•◊∞•◊∞

_____

›Mark‹

_/_/_ ©™® _/_/_

•◊∞•◊∞•◊∞•◊∞•◊∞•◊∞•◊∞•◊∞•◊∞•◊∞•◊∞•◊∞•◊∞•

The Silhouette of Time
(Moons Light)

The silhouette of time. The ringing sound, the endless light, shattering paths of forgotten nouns. A simple curse of precise beauty. Solidifying the ugly truth of loves forgotten past.

Its origin of evolved nature. The truth of fates existence, sculpted into existence by hopes unknown magnetic, mimicking, manipulation, manifesting, mind. Melancholy, meanings, mandated, monotonously, maybe, made, mathematically, meticulously, moving. Meir, micro, milliseconds, millenniums, misconstrued, maps, majored, métier metaphorically, mesmerizing, man. Momentarily, most, meteor, missed. Macro, misunderstood, microplanning, metaphors, meant, meaningless, monochromatic, marooned, mostly, manic. Magic, maleficent, moldy, members, managing, mundane, main, misdirected, misunderstood. Maine, made, marquee, mummies, malice, muses. Marauded, mutant, mirrored, mirages, muffled, mistakenly, monotone, metropolitan, maverick, midnight, Maxum, merely, mistook.

By: The Third Right of Malcom.
The 3rd "Right" brain of Man.
The lll → of a Male of human Matter
Who Splits their name →into unheard rhythmically placed, color scented, tastefully

felt, proficient, points, of theatrical, nouns,
SOUNDS Rudimentarily physical.
(The third right of Man, is to write freely).

    Just to collapse the bounds, perceived as a construct taught by human consumption of vowels.

    Realistically playing with the history, blissfully, so badly pronounced. But taught by those with tongues of cellular structure. who's dusty dayz, creates material ways, of golden empires. Of timeless efficient gains of equity.

    Fundamentally Forming Foundational worth. For they know they weren't the first, or the last. So, have only been learning to teach the taught thoughts. Of teaching one's self, to learn & remember. To pass around tools of memory forms.

    Directing the growth of the rings, of the timeless oaks marbled ripples. Like a well-made riveted, rut, of sound. Of a single consistent droplet of refreshed, renewed, hydrating, light. For so long the indentation made, creates a depth, of un-calculated risk. Momentarily bare, before seasons of sap consistent, glaze the cracks of healing tasks, tastefully paned into rivers of old.

    So, given a name of Sea Shrub {A}, and wide to conserve. But that salty H^3O of times consistent, relentless turning hours sanded, tangible at first.

Marked by suns right time. Creates just the right, flicker against the moonlit skies, harmonizing hum.

That normally would shatter glass, into sand, as coal burns just as bright, as it's willed under time tempered pressure to Yell-O-w stones found, diamond. But clear matter of shrubs we weed, materializes a new as nutrients for agar cellular constructs.

So, the time holds in place with this singular silent select ring, scabbed by bark. Whispering whistles, wishfully through falling leaves. Wondering why would anything want to remove the unique evolution of a directional, recorded skip. Recognized, as a Recoil on a Bow and bowed to stars, recollected, remembered, & recorded thought by:

The Written Pen Name, The 3rd wright of Malcom R ←→ L (Brain centered thought).

The 3rd right of man, is a given right. To a Being capable of such self-destructive perseverance. Pushed and forced as a simple droplet of needed elemental source. That matter molded, that makes up ¾ X% of ones-self, embodied existence, excellence of physical forms. Parallel in present planning.

For equality in the same precise rhythm. Thinking like a rain drops simple patterned, path effect on existence. With only molecular structure to exist outside and within its own realms.

Tying the consciousness Soul to the Spirit, Heart to the Mind. Present to Past future goals. Bringing a full extension of the 3.14 {ongoing}, Life of the rhythmic rhymes. Of the ever expanding, an impulsive precision of Universes surrounding placement of light prisms, vibrations of sound.

Tastefully rolling breaths of written vocal rounds. Like mountain marbled mazes, surveyed by bells chiming all around, as the light rolls in and over the absent space of one's mind.

Stirring quakes from the vibrations calm within the seas, with a simple calming whistled wind through the cumulus groupings, soaked up by the sun. To try to reach the driest corners of crescent shores.

So that even the darkest of cracks, that haven't been touched since it all began. Mere memories have yet to be untied, by a tangled knowledge forgotten to past muscled grasp.

Just given the chance to unfurl the canvas of creative sight. Blossoming new fields, damned by beavers' destructive nature. Just Merely shaping a new pond of existence, while splitting the first given river flow. Energy enjoyed by even focusing hope. Finding lakes of legends filling past.

The smallest of ripples ever skipped three, between all four quadrants of scenic geographic mind. Creating a unique push & pull of opposed spinning elements of past Relics, Polarized. To hold physical to the philosophical perception. Grounded by Spiritual, and emotional insight.

The only to have all four parts spinning at once, centered balance from those positive & negative balance effect on the counterintuitive axis of known knots.

While all the other forms of living periodic mass, peacefully placed within the gracefully guided mountainous moons, blue light, of hues-of-man's delight, formed through this ever, shifting existence.

-The Artist Knot (PO^2)

<u>Notes</u>

•◇∞•◇∞•◇∞•◇∞•◇∞•◇∞•◇∞

_____

›Mark‹

_/_/_ ©™® _/_/_

__Pinky in the Brain__

To truly tell my story, you must understand the hue cast upon my vision of hope as a child. I considered my life to be part of a given lucky grace.

Today I still believe that. I have the soul that everyone pines to understand. A spirit that refuses to stop in time, trying to fix the cracks in my heart. While my mind confuses the three. Like kids running around knees.

I minded to tell a remarkable story of Hope, one of the classics. Teaching themselves how to survive the existence, they are living.

An unnerving state of realization hits those who tried, to block the existence of someone writing. Their deterioration on, one being. Then there would be no such thing as a breakdown.

Having the consciousness, to idealize that thought, is what is actual, in the plan of all the aristocrats. I myself have been programmed with those abilities, of a humble sheep. While a system of genetics has kept me going. Only to show the incredible power of minding creative sight.

I am the only genetic makeup of my existence. And so are you.

I am. "The Only Original". The one who could not read or write, well. Math was beyond secondary. For I only thought of what I was told I could not do. Finding science in the conclusion of the religious perspective. Of a philosopher's sight.

But I was given love in my life. And oh! did I explode!

Creating an over imagined, creative thought of human consumption. The underwhelming immersive idea of those, to grand to listen.

I am the ghost of a very present past. I Have been trying to put together an almost faster code. And I succeeded by slowing down the idea of thought. So, it might last, existing, timeless.

"They, will not have my mind."

I never tried to be like every-tone and found grandeur in it.

The fuel given is from dreams. The original rockets to the sun, dare I say are our bodies. If you have any concept of your brain and soul. Then your spirit will control.

The Whistle

Mmmmm, breath in... Whistle.

And out from the shadows of my lungs.
A voice stuck in the mind.
Beginning a sowing song.
From the box of living dreams.
Trapped within Me.

Drowning in pain, as laughs roll out.

I try to let it flow like raindrops falling down.
I try to sing, what I mean, as the shy guy.
Choking on words with a tricky trap of foul bones.
Reminding a body of sung hums.
Breaths of orgasimsszz!!

Of padded down sound, into weathered sand.
Shimer and shake the new wave,
Through bodies,
Vibrating vocal cords
Like electric vibrations.
Echoing loud in rhythm of hearts, so hurt.
They forgot to rhyme, with another.
To rebuild the gaps broken.

Your spirit begins to fool your soul. As I mind my heart.
Counting each beat with great mind.
To shock the repetition.
Restarting a new.

Suddenly I hit the beat.
Like wind through, wheat.
I sow a new seed, a live.
Flowing through the trees.
I suddenly see, a reason to sleep.

Know-Ah Knights Might

No Ah knight? A man that truly deserves a shell that shines as bright as sunbeams. Splitting the skies of rainy fall nights. Doing kindness to a stranger. Giving new might to souls losing sight, of spirts oh so bright!

Giving what is so simply forgotten these days, a Po-Light-ness. And so, I turn my curiously checkered chess thoughts of chivalry, in its simplest form. A wrong turned right.

With writing of a "Po~LuRed", for this Knight of noticeably kind gesture, done for a man by a man. Defaulting, to loosing. And yet still finding the beauty in mishaps of life. This night this hero of sonic precision. Started off by giving the early day of sunless light.

That "Hey, think up not down, you could be in the ground! And probably better off, to be going here then there!"

Matter of fact, a positive spin, as he spun the wheel of his mighty red steal steed. And checked me back in place. And onto the board of Life!

Weather your board is checkered or decked to the fullest, of candy colors, raining rainbows, over lives under or over a bridge, trapped like a mini mammal. redundantly exterminated over histories trivial bit mapped maze.

Controllers must be charged. While steads or motion projectors given some proper romping, revving, and finely tuned up rhythms. To accent upon the challenges once unknown to all. A new page will soon be soaked in ink, for I was guarded by a man of beautiful soul, accompanied by a robin blew, of Female collaboration. Causing shyness to overcome my previously confident mind. A quick wit of fun words and spit. Briefly gestured across the travel. With at least the social lease of "maybe", might see you another time soon.

And yet patients still pursued with the kind man, I rode behind at first. Now sitting left over, to his right. Feeling a great debt is owed. And I should just thank, before walking off into a drizzly direction. Not knowing left, or do I go slightly off the upwards of slightly west ways. As another calmly timed clock marked, move of left-over wright!

Rippled through the air. I'm going to be alright. A rarity of a funny clever, Man. Keeping this mood light. Like an old friend, who deserves armor of the finest, for simply being the kindest. When a person needed someone to notice, a laugh with companied shelter from the world. With a safe trail home.

So, a Po˜LuRed is very much deserved. A unique facet this will be. Since I've never done a focus on a human I did not know. So hopefully this will push the pulling wind-z yet to pass, crinkling in the breeze.

The cell-shift of Ready to Organically molt. Molding orange snuffed noses, red with blankets from the Trees. Treating them as castles stricken with wooden beliefs. Some square off, yellowed medium of Reds hue. Saturated with random bright shines of brown rosy curly cues.

To stick to all the fleece now growing on those sheep. Clothing a whole other species, for the winds to whistle between hallowed trees. Before the spices of all the nuts are buried with the seeds.

Silent go the crickets fogged, in hoping amphibious croaks, meals with ease. Early the sonic battering wings of mammals. To fly through nights, appearing as an escape goat, for certain humanities latest reprises.

But tonight, this self-named man of winged sunbeams without sun's rays. Rarely do you see, hear, or smell a delicious trio, of salted land and sea. The meal of a true heavy hitter, out to the seas from a Long Land Isled next to new cities of old Amsterdam.

That Know-ah, Gentle-man of human decent. Oh, how God gave him, glory in spirt, and minded his heart & soul.

BRING THAT GOOD OLE SPORT BACK!

For he seems to be able, to have Knightly Glory held in a chess-met. With a backgammon kind of beat. That would tap a nice rhythm & speak. As he checker-REaD, to swing back as a Bat, MAiNily focused on painting the ball, across the whole opposing, team.

A Crack! Splat, whistle, click, clack, Splat of checkered chess strategy, so easily done, with the confidences of a Knowledgeable No.1, Ah. Did you see? He brought me home! with a happy, thankful, appreciation for an adventure! I'm glad I went on now.

For this Man parted a feeling seizing up in me. Of true human decency, nearly extinct. Noah of Light breaking through the overlooked, boxes, Check... you were a King, the night you found a lost poet, and showed him po-Lightness of a true Mate.

So that purpose was given to The Pen name, The third Right of M. A new reason to rise, to a challenge mathematically unseen. through Centric's dimmed fog of depressed, mood, hope doubted, Jack. Ever, deserved Cali along Dans failed attempt at a life. Always just a silly monkey boy getting hurt for not heeding life's warning and dangers.

But yet, armor earned bit by bit. And kindness shown. A lesson, on a mistake, grown. And an adventure, Septembers sun eighteenth daily hours, before Suns Rise yearly marked two-zero-doubled wR I▪Ght. The man named with numerous calling sounds, is already thankful for the day. While humbled by a stranger's kindness.

▫The Man of Many Names
The Knowledge Now Known.
A Thanks to Noah

This is Called a Po˜LuRed. A piece of creation that is a genre all its own. Shifting and emulsifying emotion with physical and spiritual sense of material and immaterial mass. An almost polarized vision of words, with the sense of Folk-Lur. Encountered through being, by Reading.

Signed
    ˆJack Cali
        ◇ The Lost Poet
            ○× Centric Hope
            ♡Daniel Timothy Harkness
            ☆Green Eyed Monkey Boy
        -The Artist Knot

THE AWW THE ORIGINAL

I'm running out an extreme into softer colors grown on mothers' heart strings. Only to be picked by the kids to be given the oldest rhythm of a shelled creature. That gave birth and rhythm to the same act of destruction. Of the child's birthed. The scariest split of energy of demonic power, love.

Only to be used to trap and seal the very same gift given. I saved the petals that fell through deaths gate. On times past. To simply put back the end of a perfect rhyme. Of the oldest story told.

The story of using the newly created, cracked sound, of fires on the ground. Still scaring away the once ancient man, who broke mountains of giants. As they slipped from existence, and into the canyons they fit.

On the second creation after the body of leftover pieces of scraped mass. Made smaller than most at the starting gap. Signaling the end of a five-year plan. Snapping into an existence a pure written percussion that when heard and read once changes all the ripples. Creating waves heard, like rain drops on sandy shores.

As the glass ceiling is shattered, into Jems. That mark my eyes, being wet from the soul taken from the mass of time and split into ethers, sporadic percussion of periodic, beats. R-º-R.

In the sense that even rhythmic beats, were teaching the whistle of sound that could only change into mini floods. Of the collective perfect disaster of beliefs and truths. Wrapped in the old star games, still thought to sculpt evolution.

As the rising sea pulls and pushes the unique ruder of all the rooted ropes. As the ship turns, with the metallic made notions of magnets taste. That speaks to all of the time it took. To stop the cracks man made when they built themselves to the sky.

Demanding god rights, from souls, that spun around human in retro fit, genetic cells. Called the cell bits of rhythm and rhyme.

Making mass of one's own body. Everything with the truth and time given by birth, wrapped with the accepted cells of the father sea.

Salted with cliffs of a single given. Washing the genetic sands, separate. The first women of tragic. Stone to hum the endless, song of the first known blood lines.

In which one male was thought to be a great king, calling the name of a god. Now a name of being and nature that bows to the DNA of a forgotten child.

Until the last of another, was sculpted by the hammer imagined in historic mind. Too heavy of finding, while filling all the cracks. That opened the vaults of higher powers plan, to teach the soul of ones-self.

When the towers trumped, man. Who achieved the golden task? Given to humans as something sung between minds, that the last to first monuments, of mountainous hearts.

Of the games created to play with a mirror of place holders, putting together matter with tones of X-3-in a row. And O's always to the way of, ever losing to sight. With keys that marked, the shortcuts to find the lights to the path of time.

Shooting out light rails of energy. So could step through life's door, with the demons tamed by the endless repeat of sounding time. Preferring the gravity of light attributes.

On a question, all asked. And kids would shout back into cracks, sands of beaches past. To mimic the giants that were so small and timeless in their time.

Broken until the brain, self-sculpted, as the being dragged its own body from the sea. Manipulating the pressed objects into bodies. Seen as elements of mass, had already broken in-half. Into the left-over blanks. Of man's fire logic and black volcanic ash.

Ever a molten glow of the heat from deep inside the now forming ground. The child cooled and molded his mind, and with a "thump" thumbed a print of self being, the wind chime of decoded sound. The Mind.

At times a beat I never stopped singing into the originally. Head-Drum-HEarD. As mind stretched ideas of man-made-gifts. And the sound of humans stomping grounds, filled the skies.

From child, to the afterlife. Met with growing, as forever thought light of a mind created. Of godly shaped excess mass. While given no blanket to cover, but the sea.

Quickly grabbed by the spirt and thrown around, to blanket, sheep's first shed in time. By a partial being, who's choice to let the ripple be given to all! First!

Before the path gave-way to an ever-changing base of vibration. Always copying the end-space around one's own rhythm body pattern.

To new understanding, creative elevation of mass.

Of those, ringing bells to hold in place the massive energy of centered balance spinning.

Cracked by those, of soul strength. Stoking the fuel of a ship of endless rounds.

Spinning the earth so fast, man moved freely between the life rails of a glorious green and blue ship. Sowing fabric of the universe, in a slowed wrap up to the simple pattern.

Created by a self-made gift, of simplistic function.

As one has to speak so quickly, so the line drawn in time, that was missed, Lost. In the wilting peddles of dreams to fly around the universe of perfect heat.

Evolving back to the beat, of the cell stemmed from the milk grown, in the choices. The greed of people, left a poet rarely seen. Almost Forgotten.

Then, took the embers of a human spark. To remind the stars. Now! Re-shift to my stance of memories. That tell of why an artist must be created, with purpose. With the passion, of the true loves hidden sound.

Whispered across the physical form, of a mortal being standing. Through all the lives as a skeleton, dressed with his composite, custom, sun healed skin.

By a kind of creative sign, like magnets of maps to follow. As a group broken and scattered, molded back together. Through them, shifting life to the earth, of one paradigm.

That now crashes creation, Three different ways. As universes created, by one with all its parts, after twelve trial runs, of not just years. But lives around the sun in balance.

That caused Jack Cali, to call out "I am the Coolest Cat of all! I sailed a churning mass of volcanic acts. To flip through the devil's gate, a sliver of Nordic light. Cutting in a rhythmic review."

Everyone loved the sad sailor song of the Jack that ran to Cali and back. With no-one knowing the real dream he sculpted. With no end to his ceiling.

Exclaiming! A New sound? Of the crazy centric kid. Somehow did it again. While surviving the endless thing, causing damage to hearts. The Now heard, rhythm of a man.

One Of human compulsions, to finish the thought, with names of past, holding tight to dreams and goals of personal flight. Hearts strings aligned, with strength of lifeline's Fated Hope.

Sprouted through the seams of scars, burnt in child form. As the honor in ones-self, remained a Faithful reminder to respect a forgotten mind.

Of which reading just one line of blank paper, of endless words, first erased with his heart. Made of perfect sound, to give him the end of that old sailor, of soul. Giving way to weathered and remarkable broken sound.

Only now recording tools started to be able to slow, in his words written time, as it surrounds. With one loop he lined up as the only tesseract back to his first act, of round three, Of 15.

While marking the fact he thought of it. With Thorough thought, originally perceived under trees of salted beauty. As all the lost marbles, and self-sculpted beings became, The one, The only Danny Harkness. The five-year-old, that read one line from a book, the way a being does speak, with a pattern, only they can create.

Using custom tools, used to blank the canvas that I split the Ideas of thought, up. To teach my meaning of just being a kid, with guts to talk with the words, of third, given the write. To sculpt the world around with a new sound. Since he didn't get to be a-part of the first act. His debut!

Of a:

"CALL BACK RINGER", A STARDUST SINGER"!

Who naturally sculpts the stars, with his

own back and forth, fold. Of the repetition of four future lines, of axis given. To the empty space, thrown up to the stars.

    Because his first thought, crushed through the mortal mass. Leaving his mind broken, with the explosion of his spirit anchored by soul. Of a ride, around the sun, in his solid mass, a beating heart. Speaking-out.
One, tWO, tREE!

    Perfect globes of rock, struck with fire, when flying by, with one leash on all of existence. A mortal had swollen in mass, by a single shot given, to really the coolest game played with ones-self.

    To hide a mental brick, of words and phrases. To be spit out with the original universe singing. The call back of his foreword thinking. To even the playing field. While he refused the games of kids. Because he placed himself in the center of life's challenge. To center one's self.

    That was separated, forever left in the past. The kid of Danny Harkness, the daredevil. That walked above like a bird. As the earth still settled.

9/13/20
- Dan
- The Lost Poet

-A Centric Jack tail

From the being. With mother, at the beginning and a grand gesture of a true gods power. To create a new legacy of sense for all. This one being the reins of sailing an unknown mass around the known and unknown.

While passing the trees that I would pick up with ease and notice things that friends did not. For the areas I made my never-ending, understanding of imaginary and physical forms.

Like myself, momentarily stopped in infinite time, fast enough to float sigh-lent. As a book of better vibrance that is collected, as it hits him. Since first given, the tongue of original sound to be slowed by rhythmic vocal voles.

Thyme(d) with his cells of every ether.

That friends saw collapse, multiple times. And just come back with a different line up. Of the same twisted rhythm through shattered teeth of," A, Sun-sailor!" Who cools as the hidden demon, if I would ever create, shot back through the lining of sound?

That made the man who lived it, open to all to ask. And answered by himself to him-self, in a rhythm of vibration that evolved the ears. With the sound of the food going crunch, crunch, munch.

As he wrote. Parrell of the perpendicular color made determined, to move through all cracks. Beside the one I recently wrote as a signature of the being existing, some won't even be-able to register as a life filling up. While a construct of templates, I created to spit my own pressure of fossilized sight.

A Sound of time, thrown 12-folds straight round, colored with names of numbers and generic words of langue that pings around and lines up as the start of a vault of one's own gifts to live.

They used their heart to protect, their family that had a somber child, songs and odd smart things. Keeping balance, written down one arm. With a spit so loud, his tongue tied itself in knots. Around the clock, unraveling back to the sun split, of thought.

The coolest move of the purple devils speak, of life to walk through like a story, because the life he was given was, full of spirited souls and the sounds of genetics past, to all who choose to see.

A blinded kid of 31 freeing the shackle of life really to me. I GOT IT.

But it heats up, all back into the black out of 15 and with the math, as I talk back with only sound, I have mastered. My brain shut down to speak real straight, magnets I made for the ride of a life time. To question the forward thought, of how do you bring back animals of time.

I visited my body in act 1. A blind mass but great horns. With calico marks the past he never got to sound.

Wasting the last of it on an endless verse written to a soul whose mind seems to split and sift through the endless meaning. Of one's words, finding stronger, speak and mark, in the poem of hidden growth of the magnetic sound.

Shifting the poles, with Nordic light, oh! What a sight! Shattering ice of the oldest sound, of scientific notion frozen under suns light.

Rifting between shattering ice and entire oceans called with a sound of One, toe, tap. For the weight of given love, based on not only the five fingers tapping into a rhythm of creation.

I could only throw things to the cracked other-side of a mirrored end. To me saying, if I made one demon. It would be love.

I would struggle till even time its self was lapsing in rhythm, that I would endlessly ride back, behind the horsemen of old. The "Tap, Thump" of the quickest unused space. Ever to be created, the only first made by a moving child of salt- N- sea drying out 1 {act} as a new, were for a life of legend, was a sight forgotten to the stars.

Ridding space and time, Rolled in one tired tongue of dramatic style. Where I quite to call the march 1st girls of swollen time. In my arm, writing more to a story to smart that the branches will be mis-understood. As the weather of undeniable truths. Of a mind saved, only dropping, the weight of hand-made, mic drops.

As sleep crept in to the hibernation, of the 3rd round keeping the space to those kids, who's feet have yet to beat stomps of endless star speak.

A distant memory of a day ride back from a house that I created endless, "word vomit" to caress a soul of endless. Feet on a dance so unique.

The ground magnetic, in goals for me to simply word. Historic in originality, sarcasm, my feet trip on endlessly.

To simply, simplify effective beats. But never reminding, how strong the ability. With no exact construct of mass floating, in time, as mine!

THE BONES WAITING FOR ME TO

AWAKEN AND LIVE WITH ALL FORCE OF GRAVITYS PULL!

WITH SUNS EMOTION, THROUGH EVERY STRAIND OF WELL MUSCLED PAIN. HAPPILY, SEEN THROUGH SOUL FILLED EARTH EYES.

The golden time watch and compass written to the only one, forever called back into existence. With the parallel of all the plants lined up with masses, gasses, and the treasure, of the click. Of a track being reset, fighting for original rights of humans.

I just feel the words are getting to an almost new meaning of the paths that honestly missed. Empty of sound. With someone who retained a lot of nothing, but said in understood brain streaks, back and forth between beings of mortal grasp. A poet's circling loops.

A single time. And rarely do they meet without already partial stardust I picked up into, common science tools. I just needed for quick access, of a man who skipped part one and part two and called Three. To dive into my working numbers, of given past and sound.

A recorded record scratch (a mimic of shattered mirrors past).

I have marked the adds/changes in bold, and left this unchanged from the original first write. Or "worded thought vomit". In bold are bits I feel was someone's joke, to change the structure and meaning behind the piece. (An ongoing battle I have had to deal with in a lot of my writings).

From the being with mother at the and a grand gesture of a true power to create a new legacy of sense for all. This one being the reins of sailing an unknown mass around the trees that i would pick up with ease and notice things that friends did not **like** except for the areas i made my neverending **neverland** of imag**inary** amd physical forms.like myself stopped in infinit tim

e fast enpugh to float sighlent as a

book of better vibrence that he collects as it hits him since first given **the tounge that caused the origional** sound to be slowed by rythmic sound. Timed with his cells of every **either.** One **at** which friends saw **die** multiple times. And just come back with a different line up of the same **twisted** tastes through shattered teeth of a Sunsailor! Who **cools when demons crawl up at his feet except the hidden demons that** shot back through the lining of sound.

That made the man who lived it with it open to all to ask. And

answered by himself to him self in a rythem of vibration that evolved the ears with the sound of the food going crunch crunch crunch. As **h** wrote. Parrell of **the gods made** two of **demented side lives to move on through all cracks.** Beside the one I recently wrote as a signature of the **creature (xo Creatiuon*)** some wont even beable to register as a life filling up a construct of **money created after i spit** the oil to fhe sound of time i throw 10folds straight and colored with names of numbers and **generic** words of laungue that pings around and lines up a**s thw** start

of a vault of souls hidden **for me to fatten and live in the famill who instead of a blood line round. The used there hearts to buy the first origineal family that had a god of somber child hood aongs and odd smart beings to check he** kept **the death away** and down one arm. **With a spit so lound the man went back to** the sunsplit stream of the **coolest move of new devil bones around the speak of death give a crack big enough for him to walk through like a story he lied about because the life he was given was a greedy, rip of souls handed out and the sounds of** genetic past to all who choose to see. And a blinded kid of 31 freeing the shackle of life really t me i got it. But it heats up all into the black out of 15 and the math of jumping in the only simple garbage shoot **of using thw 5th made singers come at me while i talk back with only sound i have mastered with a bran that fride and made the sex seem a true animal form as** my mind rippled back to i new his house and neighborhood. And my brain shut down to speak real straight magnets i made for the ride of a life time so seemilis in how do you bring back animals of time. I visiited my dead body in act 1. A blind mass with no eyes or legs but great horns. With calico marks of the **devil of red released** into the past he never got to sound. Wasting the last of it on an endless verse written to a soul whos mind seems to **split.the poision** into a man of a self but shell stronger and speaking the poem of **hidden** growth of the **distruction** of the magnetic sound i shift the poles **with the humans** are almost going to see. I **burried all of my other selves as the** oldest sound **pf desease** to rift between the **death** of shattering ice **and** entire oceans i called with a shatter sound of 1 toe tap for the weight of love i gave out of five bassed on not only the basses of fingers tapping into a rythem that **died with how i gave my hands of real in space creation.** I could only throw things to the cracked otherside of a mirrored end to me saying i made one demond love. And i struggled till even time its self was lapsing in rythem **that i**

wanted to get my horsemen togeather of dannys trick or treat. The tapp of quickest unused space ever created the only brain first made by a moving child of salt N sea drying out 1 act as a new where for a life of **legond** of me ridding space with my grandkids. Rolled in one tired tounge of dramatic style. Where **i quite** to call my grankids the march 1st girls of swollen time in my arm writting more to a story **to smart that the branches** with be understood as the godly weather of undeniable truths of a mind saved to only **drop the weight** of **hand made explosion** as he slept in the 3rd round keeping the space to those kids who feet **i already beat** . And they saw and **put me into a kiddle of the day ride back from a house that i** created endless word vomit to carress a soul of endless feet. **That the device not ahaking the ground beat i drove magnetic tripa around the towns that let the god think the problem was the story and how.my father never told the truth. Because. No one would rightfully do and create the time lapse that you split the goals** to me as simple words i talked in ryhmes **wifh my feet to simple effective beats never eating but still reminding how strong i crushed the ability thar** created with no exact contruct of mass

floating as mine! **THE NAME OF** THE BONES WAITING FOR ME TO LIVE WITH ALL

FORCE OF ALL EMOTION THROUGH EVERYST**AIND OF PAIN SO UNSEEN BECAUSE THERE ARE ONLY** GREEN EYED EARTH **SOLD** SOULS OF

The golden time watch and compass written to the onlyone forever called back into exhistance woth the parrella of all yhe plants lined up with mass, gasses, and the treasure of the click of a track being reset as the

maine track and the others ones you can also fully support with out rymthicly fighting for origional rights of humans of **sighlent** land borrowed for the given **game** now.

I just feel the words are getting to an almost new meaning of the paths that honestly i miss **empty sound** with someone who **we retained nothing but a lot of nothing was s**aid in understood brain streaks back and forth between beinga of mortal grasp of **god circles** a d each j. A single time. Amd rarely do they meet without already be partial stardust i picked up into medical science as a tool i just needed fpr quick access of a man who skipt part one and part two and called 3 to dive into my working numbers of given past and sound.

Opening my eyes to Bright Sights

(A Band of Bright Sights) Glimmer in my ears.

Lifter, or the story is in the soil, Keep your ear to the ground

I feel my body and mind joining again, coming alive

The tips of my fingers twitch

My lips feel plump and moist as I run my tongue over them

I want someone to lead with me as equals to tame this world

I need to be brave first...

Release the steam →

Release The Steam (A Dream).

I want to say I won the game.
I want to win the game.
Why do I think I'm afraid some-times?
I'm not afraid of anything!
I had a dream a few nights ago

I was in a SUV jeep, type car, sitting in the back.
Careening down a steep hill.

The girl driving going faster and faster, I don't even recall who the driver and passenger are. As if I jumped in the car on a whim not knowing or caring.

I didn't bother to buckle or tell her to slow down. I embraced it. The thrill, the moment. Knowing what was to come.

At the bottom of the hill, the passenger, yelled for her to slow down. In my mind I knew it was too late.

The breaks squeal, the tires turn tight into the right. The car skids, parallel to the hill. And I felt the force of motion keep going. Suddenly rolling the car into a magnificent crashing roll.

Everything slowed, I saw as gravity for a moment didn't exist. I saw myself floating around the cabin of the car. Almost instinctively moving into a perfectly straight arrow, laid into a gravity-less, coffin. And felt my body jerk and shoot through the right corner of the back of the car.

I was free, crashing through the body of the car. flying through the air, like a bullet shot right for the heart. Knowing no fear. Knowing I was dead. About to die.

The impact now my greatest release.
For death on impact to the bulls-eye of the rock, ground, hard surface, that will take the impact to my head. Like a cranberry shot at a diamond. is inevitable.

All this in a split second of time.

I grasp this memory as a happening, that in realization will set me free of the redundant life I live. As a ghost.

I died a long time ago and yet remain as though my

soul was never ripped from my flesh.

I keep remembering to release myself.
Unleash my-self.
This world is mine to grab a hold of
Tap, tap, tap.

You…

And.

I…

Are nothing alike!!!

I am the crashing glass around. Your head as death becomes you!

I am the accident.
The slow-motion force hitting you.

The time, when time stops. And is none existent.

When you're supposed to have "your life" flash in-front of you.

But! As hard as you try! You can-not remember

anything, but the beauty of the happenings around you, in the paused moment of time. As solid as mass its-self.

You try to Love, Fear, remember... Like a song heard long ago in childhood. But like the angel of death, I am. I have taken your wings of thought.

Leaving you with nothing but peace, in mind and feeling.

Come now rest.
Give in.
To the Sweetest nectar of life.
Death.

DEATH IS THE TURN OF THINGS.

TO COME AROUND.

I take you on a trip.
Through, thought.
Through mind.
Through vision.
Through sound.
A feeling of absolute.

And I spit you out.

New.

Amused.

A dream is all you think.
And move back to living your life.
A bad dream you think, when trying to recall.
A fading dream.

You forget.

And so, I come again.
At the moment lost.

You feel special, for only a second
A second, I give and allow.

 Ends as soon as it is felt.
With a whisper, released from lips so soft, so perfect.

I Win...

The game is mine.

But sound goes on...
To make me play again.

I lose.

And roll in fear.

The thought you won, like a crash. Filled with glass. Pain! Life!!

I am alive!!!

Riving in pain. Wishing I was DEAD!
I think of the moment, before the pain.
My life flashing, before my eyes.
The thoughts of family, friends, love.

"Loss" rings in my mind. Like a siren.

The Pain of Loss! Inflicted upon my family, friends.

No! DONT GIVE UP HOPE!

FATE WILL NOT TAKE ME!

I will stay! For them.

My body crashes to ground. Out of the perfect feeling of nothing surrounding.

Suddenly dirt, sand, rocks! SURROUND!

Pain, Life! Blur of things flying by! Or I fly by?

CRACK. IMPACT.

A ripple, of a sudden stop. Through my body. Starting at the top of my head, through my spin and joints.

I feel my shoes, like a ton of bricks, hit the bottom of my heals.

Blood rushing through every vein. As if all were going to burst at once.

LIFE!
EFIL.

I AM ALIVE!

Blood? Blood dripping from my head?

My eyes roll in my head. A streak of desert sand, the

road and crashed car far in the distance.

As if my eyes are free moving beings themselves.
Looking out upon my own eyebrows, hairline, skull.

Like a river deep in red.
Runs from the top and middle, through my hair,
like a flood through trees of a forest.
Down my forehead, to the bridge of my nose.
My eyes roll back down.

      How did I get here? passes through the mind. Forgotten at the sight of blood, dripping down in-front of these eyes. Are they mine?

Drops flooding the black eyelashes, to many wishes have been made from.

A smile comes across.
As time fades.
Sound fades.
The memory around, me fades into darkness.

I am alive! A shrieking voice of joy is heard!
Through Chapped, Cracked, Ripped, Lips.
I'm alive.

A last breath, of a whisper with a smirk into the darkness.

And Now I say...
CoMe!
Come.
...
Away.
Away with me.
For I have won.
I have, one life!
And I give it to you.

For a Second, you do not believe me.
For a Lifetime, you do.

                    You Win.
   I lose.

                The game is yours.
                            Shall we play again?
-Written at 22.
                    -Centric/Hope

Into notes

Into notes of simple sound. I used all your voices as a pattern of notes, in symphonies. I clogged one side of my clicks to sound, as left went right, so did the broken found. Shattering into memories, of unlimited beauty. You choose to ignore as I walked along the shores.

Even if you contained me now, you could never catch the horse men of my endless sounding soul. Written on winds I whispered long ago, from spirits rise.

From whistles fluttering first and last from my existence, in beautiful hums. Shuffled into cards, of Dar{win} silence, in timed numbers. Ripped apart by the terror of a mortal... God, demi in glazè.

Moved by all the living, souls of spirits unencumbered spirits memories. Ripped from the passage of my own made-up time. Stepping from the helm of the magnetic center of balanced mortality.

We died at the beginning sacrificing ourselves. But never breathing the gasses of the spirts unused. Given as gifts made:

4 Colored in past.

3 In memories tastes.

2 Solid as rocks physical form.

1 Lasting heart of true golden lion breed.

The first to split and twist a mirage of life, projected in a hallowed out frontal lobe. Of human machine. Clicking locks of endless world knowledge in-side the muscle, bones, and cells.

Using my given right of human thought. To ignite the sight of my spirit. While purrs of cats. Eating the scraps, of fishman's work. Showing in, the 12th month of cosmic Months.

Writing patterns in symbolic ways only meant to spark the hidden memories of creative destructive creation.

To only spend the time, splitting them-self into 4ths while using one part in a time. They found, themselves during seasons signs. To forgive, those who greedily tried to take the lives of others, given twelve chances, for immortality. Blinded by the words, unable to see. The history note, knot.

As a cat, they followed in the dark, hopped outside the city of known existence. Bouncing with evolutionary slow speed, by ricocheting a faster pattern of light, pulling the seen to a dream.

A Broad-way stream!

As the rabbit grew into the hare of dangerous speed with souls reuniting. Aligning as eagles golden in the energy of immense memory.

A hare protected by eagles sight. Aligned with albatross like fire. Wind whistled in the long ears, to the pink, salmon. Time draining out the water into cracks seen by tortoises moving at the pace of molten rock, still from the burning skin of another eggs crust.

Carefully made to acknowledge the lines cut with precision by the creator magnetically unseen. Precisely to grow the next form of black hole of white dwarves' diamonds, into rivers, biblical in proportion.

Ripping cracks of wrapping sound. Breaking the time holding the notion of round infinity. Or the eight split, of the fourth fall of work. From the oldest rusted gates separating the fifth unknown dimension. Of seeing past present and future hopes-fate. Carved into ancient protection symbols, made by kings of thought.

As the canyons shook and tried to close the four winds of strings, muscles pulled from the heart of "PO^2" lost on his own tongue.

A profound writing, who wrote words. Silly melodies marbled into memory, of tongues creation, spoken to warn of changing the passing winds. By directing all spirits to their own helm, of free minds.

Funneling through a seemingly simple place given names from all, but for me, grounded as battery steal. The forethought, of a young man driven crazy by the pain of the thought of a good heart brutally ripped from existence.

Forever bleeding an unspeakable cruelty played on a soul forever torn from its path home. With no spirit to guide it to the spinning balance of colors of creation.

A man self-named, to a future of ex-Centric behavior. Ripping the molecules of surrounding curtains. With a precisely aimed soundless scream of deaths pains, poisonous grip. On one of the hearts, he first tried to save by discovering power of the third right of M's poetic just.

Ignoring mothers loving cries. By a determined colorfully sung word. Offering double the bounty of soul and mind to balancing magnetic tables. Begging for Fate to be given a second chance, on wings given wind. Breaths ripped from lungs of a mortal.

With curses of needles, of dark demons ripping into, feasting on the heart and lungs. Taking two of the spinning coins of Malcom's minds sight.

As the man was given the burden of a pain weighted with sixteen years of pain. Measurable only by the suns of past lights, tears of pure emerald-jade. Colored scars as bright, as stars. In the form of eyes, given to a machine of simple mass. controlled by a soul cracked open, to reveal a magnificent evolution, never before imagined by forces of all kinds. Creating numbers of colored taste.

Growing as quick as a star falling. To gravity of a horrid glitch. The mortal helplessly alone to painfully score and shape. Burning their own mass, to seal the demons of loves passed. With death of suns demons. May-be seen, when blinded by the darkest of fears.

By splitting a vibrant whistle, of sharp symphonies, played using a skill only known to gods. The centric man full of hope, pulled on matter with cutting whistles from a man's heart. Cutting a path to sound through, a path absent, of light. Walking with the tools left by giants, of the first fires to light the sky.

The reminisce long-forgotten, in its young form. Making the first attempts and filling the endless unbearable cold of existence. Void of any sense of only one, existing in an unmarked empty magnetically charged loneliness, absent of time in all sense of past, present and future.

With only the existence of a consciousness, that never before had existed. A conscious created by its self, to start a thought. One could argue, had to be forced by the strongest methodical numerically absent color of an "IdeaR".

Instantly erased from existence to create the first use of a never seen again, energy of a rhythmic color. Solid as the core of the earth, if ever made into a Dimond. Made only to start a domino effect, of mindless plan sight.

Shocked by an electrical bolt of watery fire, wrapped in the minerals of first thought. Flaked like snow into a time lapse. Shot like an arrow, of simple non-existents, into the fabric of time. The first vibration, of a man, named Daniel Timothy Harkness.

He first felt the molecular splitting power of pain transformed into the existence. A game changer of mortal made twisting tesseracts.

First to be wheeled by a being using the self-destruction of ones-self. Only made by the sense of gods & the devils themselves. A sick selfish trap tricking the existence of power, creation, destruction, balance.

An insurance, a not even named, entity made. Already giving balance of endless light growing like a malicious mass. A color unknown until the end of the unforeseen, inevitable, collapse of all existing synapse of energy twisting in and out of existence.

Like a golden, thread perfectly stitching a color absent of all. But glowing with a wispy green beat. Taking shape, as a hue of saturation of cosmic relevance. Beeding time with its purity of the purest intentions. To perfectly thread an immensely, sharp shard of shapeless crystal. Strung into twine, of a searingly perfect cosmic spiral of infinite rotating spirals. A triple down on a hexagon of cellular sight.

Holding all possibilities of the greatest battle of ones-self. Only now sung by an entity, that was a never supposed to exist outside its path of explosively, endless known probabilities & improbable unknowns.

This simple change called into existence by a mass, self-evolving. Shifting a self-ending code of unknown numerical cubes, hexagon in geometric shape, Ment to dissolve, all existing end, to a beginning of a grouping.

Shifting as if an endless white space vortex, could pop into existence, with two black dwarves of dead spinning soul and spirit, defensively creating a pin prick of a force opposite of gravities effect on life.

Giving an-impossible color of sound letting a mortal being control the reins with snaps of precision, vocal vibrations. Giving the great voice of a found "SPEAK" of a tonged demi-proportion.

Cracking the first layer of existence. As if it was ice, that had just crystalized as a mass on a windshield. Stained-glass, painfully sculpted to resemble the very beauty of the universe surrounding.

Shattered by sand, sharpened into micro Dimond shapes. Whipped across the word by winds, of the worst storms, combined through all unknown history.

Shattering the beauty over all time. Making the rarest gathering of liquid. Timeless to the fall of gravity. That now exists with the weight of a black hole never seen. But heard through the ripping, of times thread wrapped around what was thought to be the heart of all existing gods.

All of which formed into existing, by a mortal cell-split. Made from those who never deserved to be the ash of golden white dwarf stars, the leftover husks of immense power. While some absorbed by simple irony of existing for greed.

Instead of the protector of secrets, made to tantalize, the endless possibilities. Of the shoe-box still empty, of existence.

Starving to death the "thought". Chained just out of reach of all existence, with an endless need for nutrients. Forced for all, of eternity. To feast on its own flesh, rotten from deaths burning disease. Of ones, own personal idea of a life broken.

The first time the waves of manipulation of broken thoughts, rolled over deserts into water, forming bricks to build absolute foundations of elements.

Used like the first to exist with power, on a minute, on an ant sized attraction, of toys to build code into black and white that shimmer color, not in your eyes, but mind.

Slowly dimming the flickering shutter of Hopes' hope to carve out a small shift in one's path. Saving one existence from death, their own.

Vibrating so violently, that a tooth chips from jumping into a direction. Bending twisting and shifting a solid of infinite permeant position, mentally. Shirring a timeline of a mortal's grasp.

A mortal that has vibrated a ripple of immense silent sound. The energy stains the very existence of the flat right up and down. All made writing of a perceptively cleaver man claiming a truly, unique breath of calming center.

Showing his true form of a once called, "Jack Cali" self-named, Rabbit of stories sung, by winds of man's words.

Ripping himself into seamless parts. In cosmic pain of separating, a spread of the known and unknown to a verbal whisper of mental provocation.

Creating a brand-new style of unbelievable flat color, twisted sound. Bouncing words, of print. Shinning colors only seen through an open mind. Centered over a beating heart of lovely salted lefts, of crossed soul rights and spirts freedom.

So. you are in both your coming life. And round culdoscope spectrum of life probabilities. Created in a spectrum of the most colorful grey scale of golden-silver.

For paths no longer dictated by the hands laying, walls of broken lives, enslaved. With blind folds of hopes freedom.

As the man uses another piece of his mortality. Splitting his mind in two and gathering his lost thoughts of one's eye. A crossed control of mind over body.

Once capable of incredible direction changes. The compass, of a Buns past a Cats forgotten act, stuck in its last position. Leaving Hope to fight Centric, for the helm of a rotting ship weathered by time. That missed their star loop, created by splitting themselves to save a memory of never seen past.

Believed by those who crossed over the timeline, of forgotten self, drained of all color. Now quickly fading markings of travels and lessons. The Cali Jack, train hopper that never came back, until the end of a broken journey of scared, burnt, and worn-out spirit.

Allowing one to be as free as possible, with a person's responsibilities, left to simply care, for the steps they walk.

A truly titanic change, infamous for his journey he forgot to finish, five years before Jack even found his name.

Exhausted from the journey of a man broken from learning, the country of freedom. Marking the cracks to be fixed in the life he was growing.

For his hope to heal and fix, the cracks in the paths, back together. Caused by the souls lost and forever searching for the spirits, they came into existence with.

After the mortals who built up mass into existence. To immortalize, the history past for those yet to live. The death, demon, rot. That is left from all the terrible this world has endured.

Jamming open the gates, of iron and steel, The lost poet of, "Dan The Man, with a Plan", the whistler, centrically hoping between the two sides created, of a multi spinning, being split into impossible 3/4ths, Seventh-ed.

Sounding off with whistles of a pattern, from an absolute middle of balance. Protecting both the demons, centered, in the perfect heaven, of human's fear. Created by the same mortals. Using Love to defend, the precious patterns through existence.

But forgotten, to a creature, evolving into forms, locking away secrets in history. Mind made ripples sounded into locked memories and muscle marks. Shivered away from the most painful thought. Of knowing they forgot, what they are searching for. Finding paths of energy that pulled their unplanned, methodical, path.

They split a mind into a "centric thought", to change and hopefully save the endless shifting present time. At least for the fore-seeable future. While in the Pisces form. Learning to swim uniquely in both directions, perpendicular to the currents pulling their life.

For enveloping, the thought of ex-centric love of given right. And to give a purpose of an "only original". Due to the infinite possibility, that faulted the mortal, demi in minds puzzled - pieces.

A PO^2, A periodic.

That quartered their life, without hesitation of blindly giving ones-self. In extremes of the physical, mental, and spiritual, scientifically, sound unknown to souls denounced to the human art of bold.

To roll into a braided life, a soul anchored to a thought, of spirited flight.

While the heart centers a new axis point, of the minds, magnitude. Given physical mass's energy expediential in expanse.

The Four splits, spun, running along the lines of earth's existence. With Wit, as a Mark of Trade.

The demonic destruction, to a terrifying thought of the cold empty loneliness of the existence known. While filled with nothing but of the paths to shape with artist creation.

The mind of a Centric man, hid the pieces in the form of a spirited image of the heart, mind, and spirit, for the soul to find. In a peculiar form of a rabbit with a shadow of a cat.

The rabbit slipped out of the doors, and into the shadows. Saving, the now split man on marks. To hope the paths set will lead the four, to the fifth point of this rarity's existence. Confused and foggy fading memories.

The cat chattering a new broken sound. The soul moved in and out of the city. Emerging to the fields and country, as a rabbit of hair speed. That disappears and reappears on the hillsides.

Keeping an eye on the gates rusted by time. And changing, marked trade, and passage of time to guard. With memory losses, haunted by the spirit of hope waiting to fly.

But being grounded by the reality and findings of life's existence. Holding on to a centric thought. Into rhythmic quakes of body and mind. And why a simple rhyme played over and over. Was a memory lock.

As the mind tries to heal and keep itself following the sun turning around. Seemingly in directions that seem different to the broken memories of youth. That almost doesn't feel real.

Scares fade and reappear. But the strength of a mind that rebuilds itself, time and time again. While the bodies were imprinted with shimmering muscle memory. Stretching and releasing the idea of tools needed to survive.

Both sides, learning and growing.
Eventually reteaching ones-self, the clicks of an echo roll. Every so often unlocking memories of the past sight & sound.

To The five-year task, to remember ones-self as a whole. compiled of;

3 steps

3 starts

3 goals.

To finish the start, of the life that broke the bounds, of the known and unknown. Releasing a lung of unheard sound. Bellowing truly mountainous yells, as this man was stitched back together. Letting loose a terrifying tone.

While a knowledge of very unique perception, was found.

While the man's heart, leaked from the shock of cruelty. For fear seems to be the first reaction, but not all is, known. When confronted by a peaceful being, of unique mind. With plans that may help, those around.

Scorned for thought of better days, with seven generations as a forethought.

Who always loses pieces of himself and thoughts? While Friends and Family where constantly picking up the bits. Knowing the man gives his all. With no care for ones-self, a dangerous trait that causes breakdowns.

Those who torcher and enslaved, used as a gambit bit to push this soul. With expectations of stealing, one's life story and work. Ending with homelessness, they laughed at their games of broken rules, and disrespect. Failing, never an option for those, who hide behind. Stirring a mind to lose all sense of sober thought. With hatred set as their goal.

Taking advantage of a mind, of immense forward thought. A gold mine! Struggling through mental MinEraLs, dis-Abilities. Perceived as attributes to overcome.

Used and abused, a mental rape. A game of jest, they hid behind, after the physical body had already been scared with such actions.

But with Words, Images, Marks of Trade, Shows, Movies, Books, Patents, unheard of brand-new thought. Always a sight on this being's horizon. Others thought easy, for the taking from a mind that forgets the hours, minute by minute. With old love still burning deep, used to fear, anger, damage and make the mind weak.

Kept up days in a row, just to force a set of lies, "look at his glassy eyes, he has gone "crazy". A gambit at getting him into a box.

While the man struggled for almost six months, with logic of sound mind. Fighting the time as summer slipped away, curled up crying, the mind games they would play.

Finding more notions, evidence, all to legal rights, grossly ignored. Made a man, isolated, forced to scream and rambled tongues of responses. To endless battering, and harassment. Sick twisted Love & Hate games.

I Refuse to let, myself change, hating those that grounded me in life. By remembering their true character, while honoring myself, not to stoop to the level, of "addicts of stolen thought" A true cruelty of human creation.

Finding his muscles, held true to the sound. And twists, of the infamous feeling. That his entire self, had been stripped and sold to the world.

In all aspects of media, art, and self-expression. With pretenders and main-stream costume getups to watch the feeds of updated torture acts.

To get him to turn in circles, or fear his past friends and family where being harassed or worse. While trying for simple human decency, seemed out of the question. Changing dates in calendars of health and mental appointments states away, pricing in at almost fifteen grand to start the summer "fun" costs.

Causing destruction to ones-self and objects of need. I was subject to the cruelest of humanities money run (while storing up "CHESTs of Nuts Creative IdeaRs ™©®".

Never given proper reason or contractual right.
Forced to be unable to complete the simplest of tasks for my own goals for self-sustaining w®ight.

As all works of original writing, where twisted, destroying the original thought, 16 years of work. Mimic-ed in time. With credit taken, of pure disrespect, of one's creative skill, blatantly ignored and made jokes, to turn him back inside a box.

→Not even given a true second edit, but all gave opinions, and never once to the artist. Just cruel miss-judgment, nasty at best. Backwards persecution of personal, spiritual, religious, thoughts, and opinions. without an original agreement of release.

But scorn for writings and thoughts. No one had the right to even judge, especially while using emotion of love and fear to keep a man from healing, while getting back on his feet.

Not once approached with a contract or apology for a man's life stolen, his essence beaten, and made to feel dehumanized, while continuous currency was made, and moved out of sight.

The true greed of what is all around. Even while he daily gave, new forms of compromise. To cease. For the bother of all this, was boring into this man's soul. Rather than acknowledging, and to stop, acting like fools.

A simple righting of wrongs, is just what was asked after the endless harassment, enslavement, would not end.

As I write, the sun comes up over a perfectly foggy meadow, with sun striped skies, of blue pale to green. And threats are heard that "they have him". And I don't respond it has been going on for to-long (Not to mention, I already have acted). "For if you know and do nothing. You are the one who is causing and furthering the problem". Six months of constant debate, full outlines of legal, bring me to this day. One I have worded over and over again. Not to mention with a photographic memory, anything said, is visually seen in the mind.

First, I do not give in to terrorism or threats, and black mail is also a trait I pay no attention to.

If any action is taken and blame pointed at me, you are sorely mistaken, for you can-not steal endlessly, and pull life.

I have been forced, to become quite solum at the fact that all legal avenues and correct callouts, of a match or two of boxing ring respect. With offsetting problems of this is over and done, to continue is just a losing set.

For the sun has risen, I have work to do. My second book, of at least five, has been ruined in unsolicited edits. Plagiarism in all accounts, and not one reason of balance in the scales of justice weigh, right to balance. At this date 10/1/2021 the towns, country, and world has seen, watched, and made a purely wrong, twisted example. Of a man that fell from a tree to find, his life and all around being a constant struggle of "what and why? Am I, being treated as if I have no rights?" With Blatant Disregard for any attempt at trying to do anything and everything asked.

I digress to the fact that I have had to put the puzzle of this absolutely terrible ignoring act, of an entire society, moving into the future. For I stated on all levels and accounts.

I do not want to have to pursue this. But if it seems I must, to take back my own rights. While protecting all future endeavors.

-Daniel Timothy Harkness

And to continue (with this broken shamble of words, falsely ruined with another's negative additives, I shall leave what I can perceive as these marked in bold, to show the difference in my writing style and others.)

As the air felt thick with the movements of past. Almost like standing in a pond and reaching for something familiar from a dream in childhood. But an unknown blank in a sentence. That at first, I would fill-in slowly over months.
Then a sentence seemed to be need.

Unleashing pages, pages of time, pages filled with rhymes, pages written to further my mind, MY time. Constructs of Ideas to form Idears, and Noted Knots of thought.

The thoughts kept probing, like old electric lines were being turned back on. Sparking and needing to be fixed and replaced.

Where wires where crossed (some intentional at the time). When unnoticed for years, some taking and comparing information would match the feeling with the rhyme.

As I started to see slowly the magnetic lines, while feeling the pull of the one-self, finding a way back. To find something. But distracted by the empty yearning heart, to just see the path to the end.

Filled with laughs and someone **I remember holding whatis left of a man** so broken, **pretending** to see through shattered eyes, **ment** to c7ry the river and flood the river I hid my latch to **the** back **of an empty** mind. That sputters words **of broken blasphmiy, everyone hears with ears**, unprovoked by the sound **I start to loose faith in the tug** of a sad **distant** song.

The song of Cali Jack.

A pirate of the tracks.

Who never looked back.

Marking all rails with broken tails.

The crazy tesseract,the man of colored dirt,

Who's lost his poets plan.

To sing it back again.

A crazy old man at 24.

His back is twisted.

Falling on the tracks.

He doesn't get his family back.

It's the Calico Jack, Tesseract.

‚‚‚‚‚‚‚

That mangy old mut, licking his butt.

With fleas on his knees.

starve Jump and Cheer!

As he gets taken away.

As he hears.
He can't live here.
He cries and begs.
It's all he remembers.
As they put him into(**Under**).
A jail filled with thunder!
White walls padded for him.
The biggest sin.

My own carbon copy, given an unbeatable task, with no help, not even a map.
I should of, ferried the souls and hearts of the naysay,
a strong man.
Forgotten like an "old friend",
alone.
He dies alone with a bird tweeting you broken old fool! your mind is all you have to move.
Remember the book about birds!
It'll bring you right back to the moment you lapsed.
And unless you died way-way-back.
The car, crash?
Maybe that was the crack?!
I feel the wind pick up one day, as my head hears chimes, dancing notes of bird's charms. As my head feels heavy. As I wake a mess. Feeling you almost died, or did I?

I killed myself in a really weird way.
Like a joker I forgot to count the missing cards.

Played on the violins of ones heart strings. Harmonized by the soul. And enjoyed immensely by spirts, mindfully dancing a mass made stomp back to the universe around. A thank you to existence. Sad, and happy, emotional & creative creations gifts. In absent cold dark. And cooling the beautiful sun-soaked days of futures pealing skin. As a tasty joy of pears dribble down one's plump sounding lips.

Only to be painted by an observer, forgetting the beginning of oiled canvas marks. Enveloped in sculpting colorful beauty to be shared with all future hearts fire. Criticism, icy thoughts, of histories drum beat, rumbling stomach, hungry to do and be better than the moment existing before.

__Notes__

•◊∞•◊∞•◊∞•◊∞•◊∞•◊∞•◊∞

———————————————————————

›Mark‹

_/_/_ ©™® _/_/_

•◊∞•◊∞•◊∞•◊∞•◊∞•◊∞•◊∞•◊∞•◊∞•◊∞•◊∞•◊∞•◊∞•◊∞•

What if?

What if I have been dead all along, all alone. Watching you from the other side. Trying to grip your hand to ground me. I didn't care for those trying to help me. Saying I would never hold you again. Forgetting that I had created a tic tac toe, of the best [Ace of ♠]. One that would change the rules of matter itself to find at least one more day.

Home has always been the heart of every word. Hope has written to hide Centric's malic, misunderstandings, to give meaning to the lost poet's beauty. That The Third Right of M wrote down, so Daniel Timothy Harkness could have control of the gold. The coolest cat couldn't grasp, without bowing to Jack Cali shooting, across the unknown nature of a loves divide.

Oh, my honey bee. Wont you set me free. By catching me, one more time. So, I can keep pollinating your flower, so pretty. To my dizzy dance. I promise I won't sting you, if you just take me to the place your flowers are kept.

Flowers of infinite beauty are blooming from my soul. Because I heard your heart beating in my hand. As the memories of tulips sprouting. Through the spring of our garden. Giving my spirit the breath of life, it needed. So, my mind could eclipse with a star, shooting across the sky. Into the vast emptiness of your eyes. As I watch them fill with my love, a unique substance.

I pull out my Heart, Soul, Spirit, and Mind. To show the gods I have nothing to hide. To show you I have nothing left to give you, besides knowing. I create endless paths to my heart. Done in a spectrum of such unanimous color. Just to show your heart, what no mind, besides yours could eventually see.

The only thing I have left. Is the hope you will love me. One day. Because you love what is left. The bits and pieces of a body so damaged by the turn of time.

What I have tried to accomplish, in this life. Is to give love in the purest form. The original form. The form of the taste of orange, while manipulating a lemon, on an apple tree. For the heart of a great tree. Came from a seed. Do I dare say a weed... so lame.

All I ever want, is to be saved. Saved from a cold night. Saved from being alone on a summer day. So, I begged too never be alone. And the more I begged. The harder it became. To just be around anyone, but you.

You, make me laugh, nervous, so right, but wrong. You make me miss the past, but crave the future. The addiction to you, is almost sinister. Greater than anything someone could produce. Pronounce. :P <3

The table of time is turning. I know my talents, But I know the dream I want to create.

To use my mind to get home, while my heart tells me who, my soul instructs the simplicity of patience. While my spirit knows exactly how many words I need to write. To get to the end.

I know such an endless pain. One that has kept me on the edge of death and life. I don't want to die on the sea.

I want to show you the home, I want. I want to know the home you want. I want, I want, I Want.

I want everything. But I want everything for a life with you.

I wish there was an end, to the story of you and I.

So, I could rest.

But I only sleep, when I'm not near your heart. My soul holds itself, my spirit… restless. while my heart hopes fate was wrong. That we are capable of creating our own path to happiness.

Love = Hope / X

-+-+-+ {PO^2 # C͡Ɔ}

Time ∑ Fate \ O

The "Blue beats green" starts to hurt. As the blood bleeds from my soul. Because of the patterns I put in place. I refuse to give up on changing the rules. Even if I created them. The understanding and dynamics can always be changed if the passion & love is there.

-Dan

12/2/2019

<u>Notes</u>

•◊∞•◊∞•◊∞•◊∞•◊∞•◊∞•◊∞

————————————————————————————

›Mark‹

_/_/_ ©™® _/_/_

•◊∞•◊∞•◊∞•◊∞•◊∞•◊∞•◊∞•◊∞•◊∞•◊∞•◊∞•◊∞•◊∞•

Red Paper Clip

What if a red paper clip, is not what you trade to become rich. But what holds the wealth of your thoughts together. So, years later an idea, can become your greatest legacy?

To create a lasting legacy, of prosperity. For genetics to grasp, concepts of broken moons past.
A triple down on the rising sea, green, in Algee speak. Broken by helix codes, of blossoming blue and energy of yellow, grown green. Of slow planted growth. The volcanic red, absent of chard black coal.

A pressure of diamonds goal & emerald copper rust. For Iron holds us empires tall. The wise beings of creation, care takers of puzzled human charm.
The star speak, of Dan's-dusty-poets, lost tongue. Guided by hopes everlasting love. Fated by a centric thought. Thrown out by a pen name, and a man of many names. A fished extension of Jack's paw thumping.

As the mind historically understood, caves we carved, and fields we sowed. By foot of squared. And root we stored. For winters could only feed so many.
With walls, we made doors, to keep out snowy owls. Giving mice, of mighty moose snarl. A honey speak. To the combs, we borrow, from fathers of rising suns. Protecting sisters our mothers desperately taught the hummingbird hum.

Golden blue and green, we flutter hearts of yesterday's sweat honey suckle, with golden rod meaning. A salt water taffy of yes, York of old, and new. A new aim at the damp swamps growing.

A levee of the lakes that bolstered rail and Midwest. Mountains, rocky spanned, with skipping stones on rivers boldly crossed. Dare I say, to the golden coast.

We shined shoes tailor made, in New England colonies. We popped fields of new crops host. The foundation of the American state. Told by many seen and heard by all. New roads of mineral shimmer. To the Azul skies.

The seas we sit between as tides grow. We know how to break waves of floods. Rivers we clipped together. With springs we paint to code.

Our paper trees moving cave lines speak. A numeric platform of new, in-&-out spatial, to those.

Who forget we did it before with star maps, and an open neighbors door, saying "hello". A sound across every language. A round kind of sound.

> -Daniel Timothy Harkness
> -The Artist Knot
> -PO^2

End Notes.

Knot!

Knot's Notes & Letters

All working data & intellectual property is part of sets of Numerical Constructive Art & Literary functions.

    This is a write on a thought, to encompass all DTH's next steps in needs, to expand at a slow-expediential rate.
    I.E., To balance the intellectual and personal inclusions, of time and effort effective value.
    ›American dialect of writing‹
    This paper is a draft of listing just a simple need of a work space for me to accomplish with a way to approach, investors for all current-& on-going projects to completion.
    ›Gardens of art to popular demand with understanding, a team effort of new growth. In guided scene to shine of mountain fields blown, beachy stamp & seals. Stamp note of worded. {poet voice}
    Mentors of mechanics, science, law, agriculture, education, philosophy and travel. With

added seats to sketch open boards of IdeaR thoughts to Creation in 7 years of working expect on the partners joining, life needs.

Choice sorting easily done, by old-new and my understanding of a sounding board. Or outside thoughts & view. Any triangle intersecting, perpendicular, parallel to my minds current sense of creative sculpting notion. Of best looping round thought.

I.E., a teaching & working board to guide. The correct avenues of current events, to help, stream a traveled magnetic line of concreate creation. With cost and unseen with sought meaning covered.

Current numerical living with the growing of # crossing deposits, of all current mental, encompassing known languages, of trade to boxed holding spaces.

Just ask, and maybe I'll throw out a Marble of PoLuReD directions of left-over wright.
Monkey boy of an Artist Ace.
Qued into infinite Puzzled Pieces.
Only questioned by stars of hearts Xs and Os.
Hopeful in radial thought.

Trademark and copywrite written, division to time.

I.E., a Rights twice peaceful pace, of Poet^2 Pi.

`Ask & May the Bees tulip, a muscle of peaceful equal marbled PO-LuRed. Marks on symbols of the artist Knot magnified by tortoise anchored spade.

Played infinite tasks of rabbits, to climb the mountainous trees. He did the run, of lock and key balanced magnetically, through the farms of springs floods. Blacking out the blank brick & mortar. To cheers to a candied time.

™ © IDeaR ® 2020 (with previous notations of past).

An infinite puzzled piece question, star HeArt notes Knoted Ex-change, numeric in contractual values of all previously stated, and documented forms.
Hope-FulL radial thoughts.

Inspired the write.

Hope you like. And there is, other words graphed into verse. But again (Thumbs up or Down)?

Just wanted to say, I understand but also just ask. Maybe I'll unfurl a note, of knotted acorn craft with a marble of Polarity.

Flat sands T R 3aSure the HeArt-mind, spirits-souled. Bright to your Self-mIGHt-ScriptArt° • inner sight. To find, personal might of soft careful physical to mental delightful. Memory of personal, growing sights of mindful sounds. Past to present future development of one's self.

Growing tendency mends, of prospering, an all-encompassing Farming-Art-to Community to Business Creations, thoughts of, finding - constructive.

12/10/202

Dear, Media

I would like to inform you, of an ongoing issue. I have been struggling with over the last year or so. While dealing with an ongoing passion to work on projects, Literary Art, & continuous designs for products, and creations of colorful fancy.

I have made a bit of a splash, walking around the towns it seems, and have been acknowledged as a bit of an odd one. I have been struggling with finding the correct terms for the ongoing "devices" or sensatory disruptors. That seem to be able to read or suggest the synapse pulse from one's self.

Seemly used to confuse, push, persuade, or generally disrupt a normal thought pattern or action. Mostly used it seems to cause panic, fear, emotional harm. While pursuing the will to steal one's personal self. And Intellectual thoughts.

Endless promises of "just do this or complete that", that are forced upon those unaware of where the sound disruption is coming from. Tonal, in both mechanics, and in general vibration. But a high sense of electrical or static up the back side of the mind.

Even at times, causing physical pain. And as if controlled by an app. Turned up and down during the operator's whim.

Multiple sets of known and unknown familiar or static sound. Causing an actual sense of a verbal preannounced.

Unfortunately, I have noticed I have acclimated to this, by talking out loud. In- order to keep a mindful set of understanding where I am perceiving the sense and/or sound.

Endlessly used to try and pursued one into a mental box, of unrest, and used by others to purposefully keep someone from general basic human needs. While pushing one into an almost unsullied state, and claiming that every choice is "Your Own Fault".

Personally, causing loss of constant "works". And an endless back up of almost two years of work. While others have acted as if, one is "lost in their own mind". Along with multitude of excuses.

I have also been dealing with personal battles I have not strayed from acknowledging. While dealing with personal recovery from physical and personal. I Have noticed almost a full self-image, being drained by multitudes of different markets, and exchange.

Spending thousands, myself to just keep my head above water, while family endlessly covered at least triple. With very valuable works, of designs (patent structures), imagery of mind, theory's, templates, spoken, written, and original creations. Nicknames, artist names, pen names, and all being duplicated in an almost fashion of cruel intention to destroy any chance of every becoming or working towards, goals set almost sixteen years in the past.

I must mention with side projects, a forming full series of two different set media productions, Pod Casts, Books, and furthering social, creative, and industrial discussion, and set ongoing building processes of a multitude of business, and overall numeric values. Rudely remarked, twisted. Without, any regard to the being that deserves at least a moderate acknowledgement of respect.

Attached I am giving a snippet of some of the work (Pink Moon Rise, Over Old Ports Bay), and ongoing notation of asking for information, the sense of misunderstanding and general thought to cease the constant disruption of my life. Two years it seems. While just about anything and everything has been dismissed by all as just odd circumstance.

Any information on how to stop the constant(s). So, I can truly get back to being myself, would be a greatly needed and added bonus. To finding and finishing a multi formed, set of interests and sights. Styled to achieve heights of ones 30s, living in the New-20s.

While I really am looking to excel in the avenues I have been truly concentrating. While recouping the general respect of "Mark". And all forms of one's rights to freely pursue dreams.

Sincerely Yours,

A Modern 20's Man

-The Man of Many Names

-The Lost Poet ∞ Artist Knot {PO^2}

-Jack York Cali   Centric/Hope-

◊ Daniel T. Harkness ◊

•12/10/2021•

Dear, Colorful Hues

"Bee Truly a Marbled Hop PO-LuRiZed Vision."
"Find your Hue of Humanity."
"Information of magnetic balanced, royal are we, working of honey pot candied thought."

Those who know parts. This is Dan coming into a center of being. Heart and Mind, Spirited with an ever growing grounding Soul.

Anchored sails and wears of trade, mending and building empiric flowing equators scaled. Bounds of balancing rainy, sunny mass of scientific religious self.

Historical, grasp on green grass to moo to milk. Ricotta to solid mozzarella.

Linked to-day's past lifting thought,

"Tomatoes and basil can't, wait to be simply plucked, with chit, chat near an area of tasking garden. Planned by stomping that old oak spot.

Just remember that.

"A-corn •◇∞• HeArt"

Ps: The cost of a 12w Light bulb + Minimum wage (with over time considered) + Theft of intellectual property + Mental strain+ Etc. Is the cost of using someone's mind (or reading their synapse) for your own gain. A billable note - Or equal to enslaving, among other charges in America.

An Idear of regulating.

Knotted
Notes
PO²

"Sometimes ears of words, can help shine a bright light on to a saturated sound. Minding my own taste torn from old writes".

Notes

•◊∞•◊∞•◊∞•◊∞•◊∞•◊∞•◊∞

———————————————————————————
›Mark‹

•◊∞•◊∞•◊∞•◊∞ So here is a space for Yours. •◊∞•◊∞•◊∞•◊∞

_/_/_ ©™® _/_/_

•◊∞•◊∞•◊∞•◊∞•◊∞•◊∞•◊∞•◊∞•◊∞•◊∞•◊∞•

Notes

•◇∞•◇∞•◇∞•◇∞•◇∞•◇∞•◇∞

_____

›Mark‹

_/_/_ ©™® _/_/_

•◇∞•◇∞•◇∞•◇∞•◇∞•◇∞•◇∞•◇∞•◇∞•◇∞•◇∞•◇∞•

__Notes__

•◇∞•◇∞•◇∞•◇∞•◇∞•◇∞•◇∞

_____

›Mark‹

_/_/_ ©™® _/_/_

•◇∞•◇∞•◇∞•◇∞•◇∞•◇∞•◇∞•◇∞•◇∞•◇∞•◇∞•◇∞•◇∞•

Notes

•◊∞•◊∞•◊∞•◊∞•◊∞•◊∞•◊∞

_____

›Mark‹

_/_/_ ©™® _/_/_

A List of Other Hopeful Upcoming Works:

Hopefully, completed in the next seven years.

→ "CoLuRounds of a Cook" Book (Within the next few months to year)

→ "Memory Mimics" Book

→ Patents (to be Announced)

→Intellectual property formulated Idea-Irls

→Pod cast

    Traveling Poet

    $\pi Palindrome \diamond Perception_x\ PolurEYZ$©™®

→Show Constructs

Centric/Hope Game show

→Bibliographies (Writers and contracts needed)

→Charities to follow, with means of success.

        →Etc.

Marbled Memories - Forget me Knots
Post & Stamp ◊ MarkArt ∞ ScriptArt •HeArt

{Knoted Notes}

›Kaleidoscope Perspective‹

Names and objectives subject to change. Upcoming, Prints/editions, subject to edited changes.
Numerical commercial graphic and intellectual rights owned By DTH and all names associated with the being of Human decent.

©®⚜™%DTH∞А№‰∞ All numerical currency established past and future for foreseeable groupings of sun lengths. dimensional definition and measurement. IE All currency of living knowledge. ∞

www.ingramcontent.com/pod-product-compliance
Lightning Source LLC
Chambersburg PA
CBHW031624210526
45464CB00004B/1729